PENGUIN BOOKS

THE FRENCH ART OF
NOT TRYING TOO HARD

© Julien Falsimagne

Ollivier Pourriol is a philosopher, writer, and novelist. He lives in Paris, where his lectures mixing philosophy and cinema are widely attended, and where he puts his ideas into practice over aperitifs with friends.

The French Art of Not Trying Too Hard

Ollivier Pourriol

Translated from the French by
HELEN STEVENSON

life

PENGUIN BOOKS

An imprint of Penguin Random House LLC
penguinrandomhouse.com

Originally published in French as *Facile: L'art français de réussir sans forcer* by Éditions
Michel Lafon, Neuilly-sur-Seine.

LIBRARY OF CONGRESS CATALOGING-IN-PUBLICATION DATA
Names: Pourriol, Ollivier, 1971- author. | Stevenson, Helen (Translator) translator.
Title: The French art of not trying too hard / Ollivier Pourriol ;
translated from the French by Helen Stevenson.
Other titles: Facile. English
Description: [New York] : Penguin Books, [2020] | "Originally published in
French as Facile: L'art français de réussir sans forcer by Éditions
Michel Lafon, Neuilly-sur-Seine"—Page facing title page. |
Includes bibliographical references. |
Identifiers: LCCN 2020022658 (print) | LCCN 2020022659 (ebook) |
ISBN 9780143135494 (hardcover) | ISBN 9780525507161 (ebook)
Subjects: LCSH: Stress (Psychology) | Struggle. | Relaxation. | Philosophy, French.
Classification: LCC BF575.S75 P67513 2020 (print) |
LCC BF575.S75 (ebook) | DDC 650.1—dc23
LC record available at https://lccn.loc.gov/2020022658
LC ebook record available at https://lccn.loc.gov/2020022659

Printed in the United States of America
1   3   5   7   9   10   8   6   4   2

Set in Yoga Pro
Designed by Sabrina Bowers

Contents

*The French Art
of Not Trying
Too Hard*

Introduction

This book came about as the result of a conversation with my publisher and friend, Elsa Lafon. It's important to specify "friend" because we weren't working at the time, we were just having dinner. It wasn't a professional discussion; I wasn't there to outline a project or negotiate a contract. It was just a conversation for conversation's sake, over a simple family meal and a good bottle of wine. In fact, I can't even remember what we were talking about—maybe about the children, who were still running around and should have been in bed. What effort we expended—to no avail—trying to get them to do what we wanted! Maybe it would have been best just to ignore them and wait for them to tire themselves out. Sooner or later they'd go to sleep. After all, that night was slightly special: there was no school the next day. What greater pleasure, for a child, than to end up falling asleep on the sofa, lulled by the adults' conversation? Late to bed, happy to bed—it makes for sweet memories. "How right you are," Elsa said. "Why struggle? Let's have another glass of wine."

A few minutes later the children were gently sleeping, through no effort on our part, without our even noticing. "In the end it was easy," Elsa said. And I think that's when we started talking about it. Ease—what a marvelous subject. We always think we have to make a huge effort in order to get good results, that we have to suffer to be beautiful and must work hard for everything, whether it's seducing someone, or learning to play the piano, or tennis, or to speak a foreign language. Even therapists talk about "working on yourself," because we are taught at a very young age that everything must be earned, that effort brings just rewards, and that nothing comes from nothing. But I am convinced that the opposite is true. In certain cases, making an effort is not just useless, it's actually counterproductive. No one ever became more beautiful by suffering, for example. Unless they love suffering for its own sake. Beauty rests rather on serenity, on tranquility, on being at peace with oneself. I'm not saying there's no point in making any effort at all, but rather that there are some goals that can only be reached indirectly. By sincerely abandoning any attempt to attain them. Without aiming for them. In other words, *easily*. Seduction, for example: what could be less seductive than someone who's trying to seduce you? It's too direct—there's no room for naturalness, or imagination. If you try, you're bound to fail. In fact, you've failed before you've even started. It's obvious: when you're try-ing to get someone to like you, you become clumsy, precisely because you're trying not to be. But the reverse is also true— what could be more seductive than someone who isn't making a play for you, who's happy just to *be*, and do their own thing? Seduction is the art of succeeding without trying, without tak-ing aim. It's a question of charm, really. In essence, it's a fore-gone conclusion. And we know it. Either there's a magnetism between two people or there isn't. So why bother being shy, or paralyzed by your goal? There is no goal, no target to be hit, no mountain to be climbed.

Take cooking, for example. Think of the times you've been chatting away to a friend, enjoying yourself, and forgot to turn down the gas on the stove. Oh well, those onions will be nicely caramelized now. It even holds true for washing up: when you burn a pan the best thing is to let it soak, rather than to scrub at it like a maniac. I'm not saying you should never scrub, but that you need to know when there's no point in scrubbing. Letting time do its work doesn't mean you'll never do any yourself. It just means working more efficiently.

I love airport books, the kind you buy just before you get on a plane, that you read while looking out the window. Books you read out of the corner of your eye, but which imperceptibly change your way of seeing and behaving. Not quite philosophy, not quite journalism, nor personal development; more like a journalism of ideas, along the lines of Malcolm Gladwell. He gets interested in an idea, investigates it to see how it has changed people's lives, and then writes an article or a book on it. If I had to write an airport book, I'd write one about ease.

Elsa put down her glass. "So when do we publish?"

This book was born that day, out of a conversation that was going nowhere in particular, over a dinner between friends. It too was born out of the corner of someone's eye, in keeping with its subject: *easily.* It wasn't a project, there was no effort to make, no prior intention, no one to convince, no negotiation. It was just perfectly obvious. It's the book you're reading right now. I hope it will fulfill its purpose in the same way as it came into being: without trying. And that you will find in the pages that follow the natural flow of the conversation that inspired it.

1

Continue

It's like it hasn't really started
ALBERTO GIACOMETTI

The hardest part is knowing where to begin. How to approach things? In what order? When you're talking to someone with a drink in your hand, these kinds of questions don't come up. You say what you have to say, in any old order. The conversation has always already started, and you just have to keep it going. But with writing, the moment you start, problems arise. I'll be honest—I've rewritten this opening countless times. And each time I've crossed it out and tried again. Everyone knows the story of Orpheus, the musician who goes down into the Underworld to rescue his wife, Eurydice. Like Orpheus with Eurydice, instead of moving forward, every time I started I'd look back, and lose the very thing I'd just snatched from the void. And yet in Orpheus's case, Hades, the god of the Underworld, had been quite clear: "Orpheus, just this once, since you play the flute so nicely, I will let you bring your wife back from the kingdom of the dead, but on one condition, and one condition only: you must not turn around to look at her, not even once, till you are back in the light of day. Agreed?" He couldn't have been any clearer. The contract included no small print. Everything was spelled out, even if the condition imposed was a bit strange. Why forbid Orpheus to look at his wife? Surely that's the kind of rule that cries out to be broken? Well indeed. But Greek myths are not just stories; they are infused with wisdom. And in this case the recommendation is clear: if you want to reach your goal, think of nothing else. Keep going, and don't look back.

Why? You know why. Because otherwise doubt sets in and soon you're going backward. You get lost in your thoughts instead of acting, and you lose your instinct. If you doubt, you fall. This is equally true for the bashful lover who falters, for the tightrope walker with his toe on the rope, or for the waiter carrying his tray aloft. The tightrope walker first follows the line of his gaze, looking straight ahead, never down or back, not even up. His gaze becomes the line that supports him. The waiter, less perilously, keeps his balance by moving forward, with his shout of "coming through!," as if magically clearing a path for his tray laden with fragile things and drinks about to spill. This is how Moses must have proceeded as he crossed the Red Sea. Fortune favors the brave. Don't look back, keep going.

*

So today it's settled, I've been preparing long enough and now I'm off, and I won't be looking back. Why? To see if it works. To see if this book might—not write itself, that would be too much to ask—but perhaps give birth to itself, by the very method it recommends. If it could prove by example that its advice works. Where does this advice come from? Not from me, I can assure you. But I have tested it all for myself. These are practical tips gathered from encounters, personal and literary, that I use so often I no longer realize I'm doing so. I've borrowed from philosophers and artists and athletes as well as from fictional characters. I've brought in men and women of action, as well as thinkers—and sometimes they're one and the same: Descartes, Montaigne, Bergson, Bachelard, Pascal, Cyrano de Bergerac, Rodin, Gérard Depardieu, Napoleon, Yannick Noah, Zinedine Zidane, Stendhal, Françoise Sagan, the philosopher Alain, the chef Alain Passard, the tightrope walker Philippe Petit, the psychoanalyst François Roustang, the diver Jacques Mayol, the pianist Hélène Grimaud, and many others. You'll meet them as we go along. In short, I've used the people and names that came to mind.

You will have noticed that what came to hand was essentially French. This is not by chance. Of course, I am French, and you have to start from what you know, hoping that through the particular you might connect with the universal. But there *is* also a typically French notion of facility. We will examine it carefully, without falling into the trap of intellectual nationalism. To be French is to be attached linguistically and mentally to a place, not a race. An idea is French only if it can be universalised. The French mind-set is open to all comers—this is its strength, its beauty, its nobility. Descartes may well have been "in the history of thought, the French cavalryman who set the pace," as the essayist Charles Péguy described him, but unlike Péguy, who served and died as a lieutenant in the First World War, Descartes became a soldier not out of patriotism but because he longed to travel and to see the world. The influential Péguy suggested that Descartes' style and ideas were irreducibly French, but the method Descartes invented to make thinking seem as easy as being belongs to no one; the obviousness of his "I think therefore I am" is universal, which is why a philosopher as German as Hegel could say of Descartes that he was the hero of modern philosophy and not just the hero of French philosophy. Ideas belong to those who understand them, and methods to those who use them.

When we say "France," France itself is no more than an idea—*une certaine idée*—which exists in the collective imagination in its condensed form of "Paris," the international symbol of all forms of freedom, the dream of thinkers and artists. This Paris is evoked in the alluringly titled *Le Rendez-vous des étrangers* (Where Strangers Meet) by Elsa Triolet, Louis Aragon's muse—a Paris in which the Spanish Picasso, Russian Chagall, and Italian Giacometti all felt at home, and with good reason:

> The people who gathered in Montparnasse formed a sort of
> foreign legion, though the only crime they had on their

conscience was that of being far from home, far from their own milieu...Paris had handed over this small corner to us...This place for the displaced was as Parisian as Notre-Dame and the Eiffel Tower. And when, like a firework, genius erupted out of this small crowd, it was still the Parisian sky that received its reflected glory.

When the Chinese painter Zao Wou-Ki first set foot in Paris in 1948, he knew only one word of French, one open-sesame that he gave to the taxi driver: "Montparnasse." He didn't mean the train station, he meant the mythical place that all aspiring painters dream of. He spent the rest of his life there in a studio very close to Giacometti's. Chinese by chance, but French by the dictate of his heart.

By now you'll have got the point: you don't have to be French by birth to be attracted to the French way of life. But what, exactly, does it consist of? If you try to define it too closely you miss its essential quality, which is the ability to protect its mystery, and thereby retain its attraction. In the seventeenth century, that of Louis XIV (known as Louis le Grand or Louis the Great), refined thinkers defined good taste with the aristocratic phrase *je ne sais quoi*, or *presque rien*, an elusive something or almost nothing, which could signify all the difference between an artistic masterpiece and the rest. Success was not linked to the amount of work put in, but, on the contrary, to the absence of apparent effort—the naturalness, the palpable ease with which the artist had achieved his or her aims. Clearly an artist does work, but like a crafty magician or a person of good manners, he or she must not show it. So the idea of a French art of effortlessness that scorns hard work dates back to the Grand Siècle (the seventeenth century) and the spirit of the royal court. The bourgeois society that came after, born out of the Revolution, logically enough took the opposite approach, vehemently affirming equality and the value of work. If you wanted to stand out you must do so through merit, not birth. So: "to work, citizens!" But, curiously enough, the idea of ease, an eminently royal notion, survived, as though the Revolution, far from wiping out royalty, extended it to everyone, transforming every citizen into a monarch. Dead is He, long live Me! Perhaps the reason why the French are so ill-disciplined, capricious, and prone to complaining is because in each of them exists a monarchic streak, concerned only with their own pleasure. Add to that gastronomy, an exaggerated sense of personal freedom, a taste for beauty, and the desire always to be right, and you will arrive at an approximate but precise formula for the *je ne sais quoi*, which gives the French soul its characteristic bite. A mixture of noble arrogance and popular insolence, seriousness in things lighthearted and lightness at moments of great seriousness; in short, a desire for effortlessness synonymous with both elegance and pleasure. The extremity of this effortlessness is "studied neglect": elegance that took hours of preparation, but that acts like it just got out of bed. The deliberate "disheveled look": I've come straight from the hairdresser's, but it mustn't show. I spent hours in front of the mirror and in the bathroom making sure I looked spontaneously natural. I've been working on this page for months, but I want you to think I improvised it in five seconds flat. True chic always looks completely natural. Make no mistake: achieving effortlessness is quite an art, maybe even the height of art. It's the hardest thing in the world. Except perhaps for one thing, which is even finer, and even more difficult: refusing to be satisfied with the appearance of effortlessness, but instead feeling it within, experiencing it, living it. Not in outbursts, brief moments of grace, but continuously, assuredly, definitively. "Pleasure is effortless and easy, but you must learn to be happy," as Gaston Bachelard said. Passing from pleasure to happiness—now there's a challenge. Bachelard was a professor at the Sorbonne, with a long white beard that made him look like Merlin, a malicious eye, and a greedy appetite for imagination, for friendship, and for poetry, which for him were the ingredients of happiness. In this book I will introduce you to his method, along with others'—for there is not just one but many paths to happiness, some of which overlap—and it is my intention, in the time we are to spend together, to point out to you those that seem to me to be worth pursuing.

*

I began this book by saying that nothing was harder than starting. And this law is ironically doubly true for a book devoted to effortlessness. When you write, you spend your time trying to avoid starting, getting lost in preparation, waiting for inspiration. Deep down, one is never ready, and never will be. This is not due to lack of courage or will. It's just the way it is. It's the only way it can be. To begin, you have to be a god, capable of starting from nothing to create everything, drawing it out of your own inner substance. There's no point in getting upset about so-called writer's block, the famous terror of the blank page, or the fear of committing yourself—starting is quite simply impossible. And let's not even talk about finishing. Take Giacometti: he was incapable of finishing anything. You literally had to go into his studio and grab the sculptures off him to send them to the foundry before an exhibition. When people asked him why, he calmly explained that he couldn't finish what hadn't been started: "I make sculpture to be rid of it, so I can stop sculpting as soon as possible." "And yet," you will reply, "you always start again." Giacometti: "Well, yes, because I never manage to start." Logical. "So far, I've never actually started... But if I ever did manage to start it would practically be finished, I think." It is clear that finishing and starting are both equally impossible. There is, however, a way around this, since Giacometti did work, and his work does exist, even if for him it doesn't: "I wonder if behind the pretense of work there isn't simply a kind of obsession, among other obsessions, with fiddling around with clay without actually getting very far."

The way out, the miracle solution, does exist. It is sublimely simple, and can be summed up in two chapters—actually in two words. If I tell you what they are right now you can close this book and immediately put them into effect, and you won't have wasted your time. I'll go on writing the book anyway out of respect for your idea of what makes a book, and for the job of the writer, but please don't hesitate to leave me right here to go and put your newfound knowledge to use and reap its benefits as quickly as possible. Out of everything I've ever read or heard, I've found nothing more useful, in every sphere of life. It fits into two lines, taken from a book by the philosopher Alain, who was a teacher, a writer, and a soldier. OK, that's enough suspense. Here they are: "The whole doctrine of action can be expressed in two chapters, each of which contains a single word. Chapter one, continue. Chapter two, start. The order, which people find surprising, expresses almost the whole idea." Two words: continue, start. In this order: one idea. You just have to continue, rather than start. Thank you. Nice knowing you— short but sweet. Good-bye. Try to be happy.

For those who have decided to stick around a bit for further enlightenment, I have a confession to make. The first thing I read by Alain was his *Propos sur le bonheur* (On Happiness), which I borrowed from the municipal library in Hyères-les-Palmiers, the summer before my last year of school. I was hoping for abstractions and big ideas. I was disappointed. It consisted merely of platitudes, life guidance, barely concrete examples. It was several years before I was able to revise my preconceived ideas and properly appreciate the subtlety of his thinking, which some people considered too well written to be profound. "No effort you make to be happy is ever wasted." You have to have lived a little to appreciate that kind of aphorism, don't you think? Happiness is easy, it's within your grasp, Alain tells us. This is not an obvious idea: our experience is, in fact, usually the opposite. We all know that nothing is easy. Don't we all dream of ease precisely because it is impossible? Feeling weak, no flair, no inspiration? Lacking the energy required to take decisions? Run out of ideas on how to solve a particular problem, or more generally just don't know what to do with your life? Living and acting are easier than you think. And this is from a man who likes to work. Alain is no dilettante, no slacker. He's a man of action as well as a philosopher. He is not telling us to stop trying, he just explains where to direct our efforts. It's quite simple: "Everything's already started, we just have to continue. Just accept yourself where you are now, with whatever you are about to do next. All resolutions for the future are imaginary. Keep on doing what you're doing, just do it better."

To be alive is to be part of the narrative of experience, to be engaged with the world. We are always caught up in the action. So we don't have to begin, we just have to continue. No need for big decisions. To explain what he meant, Alain took the example he knew best—writing. He quoted Stendhal, who, by his own admission, wasted ten years of his life waiting for inspiration:

Even in 1806, I was waiting for the moment of genius to strike before starting writing…If I had talked about my writing plans in 1795, some reasonable man might have said to me: "Write every day for an hour or two. Genius or not." With this piece of advice I could have put ten years of my life to good use, instead of foolishly waiting for the stroke of genius.

In other words, if you want to learn to write, the content doesn't really matter, what matters is writing. The more you write, the better you write. Don't look back over what you've written. Just keep going. "I noticed here," comments Alain, "one of the secrets to the art of writing. Don't cross out, keep going; a sentence begun is better than nothing. If the sentence is clumsy and uneven, that will teach you something." It's better to keep on writing than to alter what you've written—that's how you make progress.

The writer and resistance fighter Jean Prévost, who was one of Alain's pupils, also drew lessons from Stendhal: "For the writer who corrects as he goes along, the big effort comes after the first draft, but for the writer who improvises, the effort occurs before the moment of writing…We will never catch Stendhal as he sets out; he is always either resuming or continuing." For writing to be easy, the key is doing the hard part before you start. Or, rather, to let other people do the hard part. To avoid having to begin, Stendhal happily copies out, translates, goes back to an early draft, to a page in his diary, or describes another work of art. Anything rather than be the one who starts: "My mind," he admits, "is a lazy fellow, who is only too happy to latch on to something easier than composition." Thus it is his laziness that gets him to work, but the work is made infinitely easier by this method.

What can we learn from Stendhal's example? Not everyone wants to become a writer. But "never make fun of the art of writing," Alain says,

> it is a skill necessary for any profession, and a lot of time is wasted in trying to delete and start again. Crossing out is no way to avoid future crossings-out—quite the contrary—for you can get into the habit of writing any old thing, telling yourself you can change it later. The draft spoils the finished copy. Try the other method; save your errors.

Saving your errors means carrying on, instead of going back to correct the sentence you've written. You can save the sentence that isn't quite right and put it with the sentence that comes after, which might start with "or rather," or "to put it better." Writing isn't about producing one perfect sentence after another, but about correcting your first, imperfect sentence in the one that follows, and so on. What really matters when you're building a wall isn't the first stone, but the ones that follow, which interlock, as far as possible, and end up between them forming a wall along with that first stone. Continue. Keep moving forward, don't look back. The exercise of writing without crossing out seems difficult until you try it. You don't believe you're entitled to make mistakes; you think you'll be paralyzed by the idea that you can't go back. In fact, the opposite happens as soon as you accept that you don't have to be perfect. You just have to lean on the imperfection of your first sentence to make the next one emerge. You're freed from the anxiety of always having the possibility of retracing your steps. There is something liberating about the irrevocable. Don't get me wrong. No one's asking you to be perfect—just act as though you are. Suspend judgment on what you've done and free yourself from it by moving forward. Then the rule against turning back ceases to be like the threat made by Hades and becomes the most beautiful promise you can make to yourself. It becomes a gift, for in eliminating the possibility of going back to undo what you've already done, you allow yourself the possibility of inventing something by carrying on. We learn to write by writing, not by deleting. And this method creates its own momentum. Since we have no choice but to go straight ahead, we suddenly find we are launched. This characteristically French habit of writing without crossing out, of improvising as you go and not looking back, is cavalier in all senses of the term: it drives the sentence on, like a spirited horse, granting it the right to overthrow the rules. Imperfection ceases to be a problem, and instead becomes a launching pad. Try it, just for yourself. Don't show anyone. Write without looking back. In black ink, no rubbing out, no crossing out. Let me know how you get on.

If you don't like writing, think of it as an exercise in mental muscle-building. Force yourself, if need be, and once you've experienced the freedom of not rereading your own words, you'll be in a position to do something similar in your life. Your whole existence will start to feel like it's happily and comfortably improvised, rather than straining for a paralyzing degree of perfection or giving in to the feeling that it's "too late." We feel able to make anything because we know we will always be able to remake ourselves, and that true action lies in continuation rather than in rupture; a flowing stream as opposed to a radically new beginning. Big changes often happen indirectly, through the accumulation of tiny decisions. Continue what you're doing, just do it better, rather than starting afresh every other day: the end result will be both more spectacular *and* sustainable. Don't make a clean sweep, don't wipe all your pieces off the board. Of course, it's tempting. But surprise yourself, and keep the game going, instead of turning your back on it. You can always start again once it's finished. For the time being, ask yourself what move is possible—even if it's only a tiny one—in order to enjoy the game and make it interesting.

The main error is to wait around doing nothing, holding your pen, or with your life on hold. Patience is a virtue, but there is a negative form of expectation—namely, expecting too much of yourself. Nothing grows through that kind of waiting. If you don't know how you can get out of this kind of stagnation, do what Stendhal did: borrow your first sentence or your first action from someone else, and continue it. Continuing allows you to ride on other people's momentum instead of having to use your own. In cycling they talk about "drafting," or, more commonly, "slipstreaming." In life, as in writing, you first need to get into the wake of someone or something else. We start off learning a language by imitating others, learning by rote. Bit by bit, without realizing it, we end up creating our own slipstream and speaking the language. We write, we pedal, we gallop. We're off! We never actually had to start and now that all we have to do is keep on going, it's a whole lot easier. A sculptor needs clay or stone to model or sculpt; he can't do it out of thin air, from nothing, *ex nihilo*. Perhaps when Giacometti gives himself over to what he calls an obsession, content just to fiddle around with clay without actually achieving anything, he hasn't really begun yet, but that doesn't stop him from carrying on. He may always feel he's failed to do what he was trying to, but his work gives him great pleasure. Here, in an interview given at one of his exhibitions to the insightful documentary maker Jean-Marie Drot, he has the final word:

"Giacometti, when we last met in Paris, you were making sculptures. And now in Zurich you're a bit like a shepherd surveying his flock. They're everywhere. How does that make you feel?"

"Yesterday, when I saw the exhibition, I thought it looked great. For a moment, anyway. Too good, actually. That does worry me a bit."

"Why's that?"

"Because if I went on feeling as satisfied as I was yesterday, that would mean—in contradiction to what I generally think, wouldn't you say?—that either I've lost my critical faculty or I've now come to a point where there's nothing left for me to do."

"Even so, it's a bit like seeing your whole life in one room."

"I suppose so, but it's...well, in a sense, it's like it hasn't really started."

2

Start

The key to action is getting down to it

ALAIN

Taking the first step: anxiety of all lovers, nightmare of all tight-rope walkers. "I wouldn't be able to walk on that wire if I wasn't sure before taking the first step that I could do the last...It's very close to religious faith." Who's saying this? Philippe Petit. Who's Philippe Petit? The best way of introducing him would be to make you *feel* what he does. So let me suggest a little thought experiment. At the end of this paragraph I want you to close your eyes, count to ten, and open them again. Here we go.

*

You open your eyes and all around you is sky. A bird glides somewhere on the edge of your vision, way up high. What's that deafening sound? It's your heart. There's a trembling in your legs. You look down. There at your feet—a giddying drop. You're right on the edge of the void. You lean out to take a look around. Four hundred and ten meters below you, almost half a kilometer, the length of four soccer pitches end to end, a hundred meters more than the Eiffel Tower, six times the height of Notre-Dame, your eye meets the ground. Where, perhaps, if you're not very careful... Where's that wind coming from? It's the wind of your thoughts. The only wind that could topple you. You lift your head, look straight ahead. The line of your sight follows the line you're about to walk across. Because you're going to walk across this rope that's slung more than 400 meters above the ground, this rope, or, rather, cable, sixty meters long, that you spent the night stretching out, in top secret, with your accomplices, Jean-François, Jean-Louis, and Albert, between the two towers you've been dreaming of for years now, two towers you've sworn you'll walk between one day. One morning. This morning. It's not yet 7 o'clock, it's August 7, 1974, and far beneath you, miniature workers are returning to their offices, crossing paths with the night shift as they return to their beds, and you're all alone up here, preparing to return to your rope. New York is waking, but you haven't slept all night. Ready? Are we ever ready for a stunt like this? You're about to cross the void between the Twin Towers of the newly built World Trade Center. After years of preparation, hesitation, and organization, your hour has finally come. Right now you're

Philippe Petit, but once you've taken your first step, you'll be the *tightrope walker.*

The conditions are far from ideal. There are clouds. It could rain. Perhaps a bit too much wind. It's *so* high. In *Traité du funambulisme* (On the High Wire), Philippe Petit says: "You must not hesitate. Nor should you be conscious of the ground. That is both stupid and dangerous." Will the cable hold? Should you reschedule, put it off? Impossible. In one minute the elevators will start working, in two minutes the first workers will arrive on the roof. The police will not be far behind. There's the elevator wheel starting up. Your friend and accomplice Jean-François, who could get arrested and imprisoned for helping you, gives you a look, and hands you the 55-pound pole you need to make your crossing. You can't turn back now.

OK. Place your left foot delicately on the rope. Your weight should remain on your supporting leg, the straight one, that's still planted on the solid ground of the south tower, safely on the building. Now you have to shift the weight of this leg onto the other one, taking the first step onto the rope. There comes a moment where you have to decide. The first step is a point of no return.

The first step is terrifying. Impossible. You think back to the first time you saw the towers. It was six years ago, a photo in a magazine in the dentist's waiting room. You ripped out the page and left without having your tooth pulled, running off with your treasure. The towers didn't exist yet, but you could dream them up. The second time you saw them it wasn't in a photo, but for real. From down below, obviously. Their mass, their density, their great threatening height. The photo had set you dreaming, but the reality crushed you. Every fiber of your muscles, every cell in your body, every shudder of your skin cried out, in that silent language you understand better than anyone, that it was impossible. Besides, despite all these months of preparation, it's still impossible. Which is why (and this too you understand better than anyone else in the world) you're going to do it. But not just any which way. Your first step has to be right. Or it could be your last. "The mistake is to leave without hope, without pride, to throw yourself into a routine you know will fail." Once the dice are thrown, it's too late to go back. Everything is determined in advance, in how you throw them, how you throw yourself into it. It all depends on the hope you put into it. The pride. And this pride isn't really a thought, it's a position, a way of standing tall in the face of the world. It's not a thought that you have, it's a thought that you *are*. A thought that in fact spares you the trouble of thinking. Because if you think about it for a moment, it's a crazy idea, to risk your life on a rope stretched between the two highest towers in the world. That's exactly what it is. The tightrope walker is an idea up in the air, hanging by a thread, hanging by faith alone. "When I step onto the rope, I do it with a sense of certainty." Where does this certainty come from? Hours of training, of course, of meticulous preparation, confidence in the strength of your legs, the skill of your feet. But deep down, it comes from nowhere.

The tightrope walker's certainty is in fact arrogance, innocence, or madness. A faith without God. Faith in the gods in his legs and his feet. Pure faith.

Just one more moment before you step out. Be careful how you start. Even beyond the question of life or death, the style of your first step determines the style of the whole crossing.

> To put your whole foot on the wire all at once produces a sure though heavy kind of walking, but if you first slide your toes, then your sole, and finally your heel onto the wire, you will be able to experience the intoxicating lightness that is so magnificent at great heights. And then people will say of you: "He is strolling on his wire!"

This is the heart of it: to give the impression that you're simply going for a walk, easy does it, when in fact you're walking on a rope 110 floors up. You're a metaphor, an inspiration, a dream come true. You're living the dreams that are dormant in those humans down below. To accomplish a dream, you need the lightness of a dream. So be very careful with that first step.

As we've seen, once you've started, you just need to keep going. The stones you've laid in a wall give you the shape of the stones you're going to have to put in next. The more the wall grows, the less room there is for hesitation or chance, the more you are bound by necessity. But how can you dare to start? Laying the first stone may be no big deal, but taking the first step…Freedom is dizzying, and the infinity of possible outcomes is a promise of failure, a sky without stars, a metaphysical void studded only with questions: why do this and not that? Why go this way, not that? At least a tightrope walker knows which way he must go. Straight ahead. Sixty meters of cable. The route is laid out. He hesitates not over the direction, but over how to take the first step. No more choices after that. This is not the case in all activities, obviously. The tightrope walker is an extreme case, a metaphor for all the rest. The way you start, in whatever field of activity, contains the seed of future success or failure. It's not enough just to set out—you have to set out confidently. Whether in horse riding, running, work, or love, the first step dictates whatever comes next. If you set out confidently your chances of achieving your goal are infinitely greater. A bit like in archery: an arrow that is fired cleanly has already hit the bull's-eye; its flight is already accomplished at the instant it leaves the bow. This is not a matter of predestination: until the moment it's released, the arrow is going nowhere. Nothing is laid out in advance, but the endpoint of an arrow's flight is inscribed in its beginning, and for the archer there is a way of beginning the movement that guarantees it will end well. To start out well is to end well, in the same movement. You mustn't try. You must succeed the first time. And therefore, until you feel the presence of the endpoint, until you feel you've reached it, you can't actually begin. You could, you should, but still you hesitate.

Indecision, Descartes used to say, is the worst of all evils. How is it to be avoided? André Gide, another great admirer of Stendhal, wrote in his diary: "Stendhal's great secret, his special trick, was to write straight off... This gave his writing a certain wide-awake, 'got-it-first-time' quality, something unexpected and sudden... If we hesitate, we are lost." A profound remark. We do not hesitate because we are lost, but are lost because we hesitate. You're really lost not when you don't know where you are, but when you don't know what to do next. It's easy to see why Stendhal fascinates writers so much. They all understand how hard it is to start, and there he goes, throwing himself at the ink without a moment's hesitation. As Napoleon threw himself into battle. Or as you must throw yourself into the water to learn to swim. Walking, in the same way, involves setting off, beginning to fall, correcting the fall to convert it into energy and then into a forward movement. In order to learn to walk, you need to risk a fall, to set out without hesitation.

That's all well and good, but if you did get lost, in a forest, for example, with no signal, no signposts, and no directions, wouldn't you hesitate? Descartes suggests in his *Discours de la méthode* (Discourse on the Method) that when a person's understanding has no impact on their will, the best thing is to imitate

> those who, on finding themselves lost in a forest, don't wander around in circles, this way and that, nor come to a halt in one particular spot, but just keep walking in the straightest line possible toward their given destination, refusing to change direction for unimportant reasons, particularly since it was only by chance they chose that destination in the first place: by this means, even if they don't get to

exactly the place they meant to, at least they will eventually get somewhere where the likelihood is they will be better off than in the middle of a forest.

When you really have to act, and you don't know what to do, and have no way of finding out, it's better to choose a random direction and stick to it than to turn back or stay put, hesitating indefinitely. In certain situations, choosing randomly is better than not choosing at all. It you choose to follow that direction you are only temporarily lost. In choosing, we find a way. Descartes: "My second maxim was to be as firm and resolute in my actions as I possibly could, and to follow dubious opinions, once I had made up my mind to do so, with as much vigor as if they had been convictions." A strange recommendation, coming from a rationalist philosopher. What he is saying is that the content of a decision is unimportant, once you've decided it's the right one. The truth of an opinion, however dubious, is unimportant, if you're convinced it's true...How could such a great thinker, a sworn enemy of prejudice, recommend such a renunciation of truth? It's scandalous and absurd. You can't simply decree that an opinion is true—you need first to examine it from every angle, weigh the pros and cons, take all the time you need, before affirming it. This is true in the realm of thought. But in the realm of action it's false. In practice, time is short, my friends, the sun is setting, it's going to rain, we've got no water, we must press on. In most cases it's less a question of acting than it is of reacting—to circumstances, to events, or to other people. If you spend time weighing all the possible options you might take you will never act and it will always be too late. So it's better, Descartes is telling us, to choose randomly than not to choose at all. What makes for a good decision is making it, and sticking to it, as if it were the best one possible. In that critical moment of action, it's always the best one possible. Why? Just because. Once a decision has been made, it must be considered irrevocable. So you tell yourself there is no going back, no regretting, or, worst of all, changing your mind in midstream. The true enemy of action is doubt.

So you don't begin an action because you've thought about it long enough to judge that it's the best of all possible choices, but because indecision is the worst of all evils, and there just isn't time to examine them all. Seen like this, beginning is the key to completing. It means forgetting about deliberation, hesitation, and calculation and just getting on with the job. Not tomorrow, not later: here and now. Don't wait for the first of January to make your vows. Alain says: "Making a resolution means nothing; taking up a tool is what's needed. The thought will follow. Consider that thought cannot guide an action that has not been embarked on." So you don't have to renounce all thought when you act, but you must think only *inside* the action, at its service, and only when necessary. Thought must be as light as possible, it must not trip you up. When it is regulated by action, thought is a powerful tool. Left to itself, and to doubt, it will be your scourge.

Of course, it would be infinitely preferable if we had the time and the capacity to weigh our choices exactly, like the philosopher Leibniz's omniscient and decisive god, whom Voltaire makes fun of in *Candide*: the idea that He calculated all possibilities before bringing into existence "the best of all possible worlds." But as humans we usually have to act without full knowledge. Why? Descartes explains clearly. When we consider God—by which I don't mean the god of religion, the object of belief, but an ideal being who exists hypothetically—everything about him is infinite: his understanding (capacity for thought), his power (capacity of action), his will (capacity for affirming or denying). A perfect being can think all things, do all things, will all things: he is omniscient, omnipotent, and possesses infinite will. We poor mortals, on the other hand, are blessed only with finite understanding and finite power, but by some sort of miracle we enjoy, like God, infinite willpower. We can't understand everything, or understand lots of different things at once; we can't do everything; but we are free to wish for everything. Although we are metaphysically powerless, we have something of the infinite in us. This is why, even if we are by nature ignorant of the future, and incapable of considering all possible choices in advance, we can still make decisions and act. Alain, who is an intellectual descendant of Descartes, says this very clearly: "it is pointless to think about what one is going to do until one has begun. It would be like organizing a filing cabinet before you knew what papers you wanted to put in it. Or else, like wanting to know what you're going to say before you say it." And this last example is the best, because we find it shocking. Our thinking isn't made to set out first; people who think out their actions never actually act. The Himalayan mountain climber can teach us something here; if he just sits looking at the mountain he will never find his way up it. "The reason I walk is to find out which way to go."

It's an immense paradox, but it's also the real secret of all men and women of action: they do things precisely because they don't know what they're doing. They have a rough idea, of course, otherwise they'd never get going. But if they knew completely, they would no longer need to do it. They don't act on knowledge; they act in order to acquire knowledge. They are their own first audience, as though they are observing their lives from the outside, even while steering them. The joy of action is in surprising oneself, in discovering both what is only possible because of action—a new path for the climber—as well as what the action reveals about oneself—courage, fear, etc. When we act, we are always the first to be surprised by the result of our action. This doesn't mean we have to be passive. On the contrary, by paying attention to what is happening to me I can alter my course and make new decisions, just as a sailor constantly adjusts to the wind and the waves. Acting doesn't mean making one large, irrevocable decision, but rather constantly making small decisions, according to the knowledge we either do or don't have. To do is to never-stop-doing, and to always be trying to do better.

Surely, we might think, this contradicts Descartes' recommendation that we should choose one opinion or direction, randomly if necessary, and never deviate. Is it better to decide on something once and for all and to stick with that decision no matter what, or should you constantly reevaluate your decisions, changing direction with the tide and flow of events? It depends. If all is dark around you, if you have no idea which way to go, then you must apply Descartes' maxim: make a random choice and stick to it. But if you have a few clues about the situation, if, like a good sailor, you know how to read the wind by looking at the water, if you can make predictions based on your own understanding, then you must do what you have to do. To clarify, Alain takes this example, which is the best one I've found because of its shock value: I discover what I want to say, he says, when I open my mouth. This runs counter to our received ideas, and to the popular wisdom that says you should think before you speak for fear of saying something stupid. Is this tantamount to saying that before opening our mouths we should have no idea what we're going to say? Not exactly. But speaking is an adventure too. An adventure in which we all constantly take part. When we start speaking, we often don't know exactly what we're going to say. And this isn't a defect: it is in the very nature of the spoken word. That's what speech is there for: to teach us what we think by making it real to us, and therefore open it to being redirected, modified, or corrected like any other living thing. The paradox here is that you mustn't think too hard about what you're going to say if you want to say it well. Anyone who thinks too much about what they're going to say will fail to find the words for it, because they'll be too busy looking for them. Thought tends to block words. Inversely, people who pay too little attention to what they say are likely to be carried away by the sounds of their words to the detriment of their meaning. In speaking, it is important both to let oneself go with the rhythm of the phrase one has begun, and to control its rhythm, in order to guide the *flux* of the words. Language must flow. And if the only way to say what you have to say is to find out in the saying, then you must first begin. Even when we think we know exactly what we mean to say, the way of actually saying it is discovered by speaking, with a certain nonchalance that is somewhere between sleepwalking and tightrope walking, maintaining a subtle balance between intention and meaning, out there on the rope.

Successful improvisation is thus a waking dream, and you must never think too hard about your idea if you want to express it. When you speak you must be careful of what you say—not fearfully, like children, who are told to think before they speak, nor like victims of *omertà*—but in the noble sense of the tightrope walker who advances along the rope without thinking too much about it, in case thinking makes him fall. Even if the rhythm of your speech pulls you along, it's important not to get carried away by it. To talk is to surf on one's words, which unfold just ahead like a wave, a wave that both carries us and threatens to submerge us. The speech of politicians is "wooden"—heavy, rigid, dead—whereas the heroes of the living word take their chances on as light and flexible a board as possible. People's attention, when we speak, is not directed at something that already exists, but at a reality that is being formed at every step—every *word*—of the way, right in front of us. You get the idea: if we never spoke until we knew what we were going to say, we'd never begin a single sentence.

It's exactly the same with living. There is no preparation for life. So you need to skip the warm-up. Watch your attitude. If you set off without a safety net, proudly, you learn how to live just as you learn how to ride a bike or a horse: by accepting the propulsion offered by life itself. Living like this is constantly surprising...OK, but in a good way or in a bad way? Nothing's ever exactly what you thought it was going to be. You're never adequately prepared. But the longer you hesitate, the harder it will be. Don't wait until you're sure before you act. What's going to happen in the future? You'll have to get there to find out.

*

Meanwhile, let us return to Philippe Petit, August 7, 1974—at the moment when the elevator wheel starts to turn, his friend Jean-François passes him his pole, and he has only a minute left in which to decide if—for all his tiredness and fear—he's going to go for it, or not:

> An inner howl assails me, the wild longing to flee.
>
> But it is too late.
>
> The wire is ready.

My heart is so forcibly pressed against that wire, each beat echoes, echoes and casts each approaching thought into the netherworld.

Decisively, my other foot sets itself onto the cable.

[...]

Inundated with astonishment, with sudden and extreme fear, yes, with great joy and pride, I hold myself in balance on the high wire. With ease.

3

The Temptation of 10,000 Hours

To make an effort is to work at odds with oneself

ALAIN

Ease, or "facility," is not a concept—it's a feeling. A feeling we have, or can give. At primary school, I was said to have "facilities," because I liked reading. I loved it. In the last two years of primary school I read at least a book a day. There was nothing praiseworthy in this: it was like eating sweets or being given a reward—it was literally a piece of cake. I saw my friends struggling to read one book a week, while there I was, having a great time knocking back a couple a day. Sometimes I'd read the same one twice. I remember, I read *The Call of the Wild* three times in one day, each time faster than the last. I loved the story of the dog, Buck, who is kidnapped, and overnight goes from the easy existence of a domestic dog to the cruel life of a sledge dog. Despite his "bourgeois" origins, Buck has an advantage over the other dogs: he enjoys dragging the sledge and fighting to be first. For the others it's an effort but for him it is a joy. It comes instinctively, hence the title of the book. The others suffer, but for him it is painless, it's the call of the wild. For me it was the call of the book. There was nothing laudable about Buck, nor about me. We were both doing what we loved most in the world.

A few years later, when I was in advanced math, I realized what it was like to be on the *other side*. The lesson went so fast I got a pain in my wrist just from taking notes. After two relentless hours of copying down symbols and equations I didn't understand, I felt like a donkey going around in circles, attached to an endless turntable, producing nothing but a feeling of futility. Or like Sisyphus, who Albert Camus said we must suppose is happy, even though he is condemned by the gods to push an enormous boulder up a hill, watch it roll back down, and push it back up again for all eternity. Once the day's lessons were over, the real day began: each of us, in our dormitory room, sweated over the exercises for the following day. All the "molies" "delved." "Molies" (the image speaks for itself) in "mole class" (advanced math) dug away, never seeing the light of day. "To delve"—the word has a flavor of medieval labor. After all, we were in the university quarter, at Louis le Grand lycée, and it was meant to be hell. Well, not for everyone. There were a few people for whom it was a walk in the park. Cédric, for example, who never "delved" and spent his life wandering in the corridors. A "mole" would stick his head out of his hole and hand him a piece of paper saying: "Cédric, I've been doing this for two hours, it's impossible." Cédric would glance at it, do a quick turn up and down the corridor, and a minute later would say with a smile: "There are two solutions. The second one is more elegant." He hadn't made any effort. He'd just seen the solution. Solutions, even. Where others looked without finding even one, he found two without even looking. Math was in his blood, it was his call of the wild. Once I'd seen that, I didn't hesitate: I returned to my own calling. The headmaster was happy for me to take my classes preparing for the École Normale Supérieure in the humanities stream, or *khâgne*, as it's called, a French reference to the knock-knees of people who spend too much time reading. Going from being a "molie" to being a *khâgneux* was not going to change how much sport I got to do a week, but in any case I was going home, back into my element. The teacher simply remarked: "I told you so." He knew what he was talking about.

After only two weeks of advanced math, I already felt tired, empty, short of energy, exhausted before even starting the race. From the moment I knew I had got into the humanities stream I sprang back to life, once again full of energy, enthusiasm, and joy. Not for long, obviously, since the "preparatory class" is still essentially an ordeal, but the first few days were euphoric. I understood what was written on the board; the teachers were speaking my language again. Everything was back to normal, and although the general atmosphere was stressful, understandably so in a class aimed at preparation for an exam, I felt like I had escaped from prison, or slipped away from the hell of forced labor, and could once again look out onto wide open spaces and all the possibilities they contained.

*

I rejected the suffering that comes from pursuing a path to which one is not suited. Effort against the grain is exhausting. It's a sign of courage and of abnegation, but above all it's a sign of self-deprivation. A negative virtue is not without value, but in the end someone who doesn't like what they do will never go as far as someone who enjoys it. The former will do everything on sufferance; the latter will do it with joy, including suffering if necessary. A characteristic of a good sledge dog is that he enjoys pulling a weight for hundreds of kilometers. You don't have to push him to do it. Eric Morris, a specialist in these matters, explains that to train sledge dogs to go very long distances, as in the Iditarod, known among enthusiasts as the "last great race on Earth" (over 1,500 kilometers through the cold, long nights of Alaska), there's no point in using food as a reward. Negative reinforcement, a training technique that consists not in giving a reward but in taking away a punishment, doesn't work either. "To go that distance, it's like a bird dog sniffing down a pheasant . . . it has to be the one thing in their life that brings them the greatest amount of pleasure. They have to have the innate desire to pull [the sledge] . . . and you will find varying degrees of that in different dogs."

When I read that in David Epstein's excellent book *The Sports Gene*, my first reaction was to bay for blood, or rather to howl at the moon. I was shocked by the link he made between rearing sledge dogs and training high-level athletes. When people suggest naively that you just have to want something in order to succeed, Epstein replies, on the basis of sound research, that it's not that simple. Some people can do things even if they don't want to, they don't have to try, nor even to make a decision: they have no choice, they just have to run. He takes the example of Pam Reed, an ultrarunner who participates in events such as the Badwater Ultramarathon, a 135-mile race starting in California's Death Valley, which she has won twice. She explains that if she doesn't run at least three to five times a day, for a total duration of at least three hours, she doesn't feel good. As she gets older, she manages to stay still for longer periods of time, but she still finds sitting uncomfortable. Françoise Sagan is the same, but with reading. The writer, who published her most famous work, *Bonjour Tristesse*, when she was just a teenager, says: "I read all the time, even when I'm writing. When I've been working for several hours without a break, I take a rest and read for a bit. Handing over your thinking to someone who'll think for you, especially if the book is really gripping, is the best kind of relaxation for me. I love it, and it makes me feel optimistic." I am sure that for Cédric, a day without math is equally unimaginable. None of these cases has anything to do with will, or scarcely anything; no effort is required, in the disagreeable sense of the word. Sagan, whether she is reading or writing, is in her element with words. Cédric's not just in his element with mathematical problems, he's wallowing in it. Both of them are like fish in water. Or rather like sledge dogs in the cold and snow. This is a better image, because even when it's hard for them, they love it. They love dragging their sledge. That's the difference.

Whenever I'm able do something without any effort I start to think it is inherently easy, that anyone should be able to do it. This is called the expert's illusion. The minute you find yourself on the other side of expertise you realize it is an illusion, and that what is easy for one person isn't necessarily easy for another. You find the illusion of the expert with literature teachers who think everyone must love reading. Or with math teachers who can't understand why you don't understand. This is the only thing they find difficult: understanding that what is easy for them is difficult for others.

The inverse also exists—thinking that because something looks easy for others, it will be easy for me. This is the illusion of the beginner. Just because you've seen Philippe Petit walking effortlessly on a rope doesn't mean you can do it yourself. And watching Cédric solve a math problem in thirty seconds doesn't mean you'll be able to do it too, through contagion. Generally speaking, it becomes clear pretty quickly: the beginner's illusion does not survive the experience of reality. But there is still such a thing as beginner's luck, the luck you have when you manage to do something difficult at your first attempt, precisely because you don't yet realize it's difficult. The first time I touched a basketball, I tried, for a laugh, to put it through the hoop from the middle of the court, backward. Impossible, obviously. All the real players laughed at me. I threw the ball behind me, as far and as high as I could, and just had time to turn around to see the ball completing its perfect flight and passing through the hoop without touching the edges. Then I quit the court, nonchalantly, while all the players stared in amazement. I was pretty amazed myself; I knew I hadn't done it deliberately and that I would never be able to do it again. Beginner's luck, by definition, never lasts. The first time is magic; you are able to do amazing things that are then wiped out by your second or third attempts, but the memory can work like a promise: if you train for years on end, you might rediscover the luck, the innocence of the beginner. The expert is someone who has finally succeeded in recovering the state in which miracles happen, and which is properly called grace.

Grace is what Philippe Petit displays on the wire, or Zinedine Zidane on the soccer pitch. Anyone can see it. In the case of Zidane, even his teammates noticed it. Even the wives of his teammates, despite being surrounded by world-class quality: Victoria, the wife of David Beckham, Zidane's partner at Real Madrid, compared him to a ballerina. It was a compliment—she herself was a dancer. But there is a fundamental difference between soccer and dance: the soccer player is not simply seeking to create a beautiful movement, he wants to win, and to do so he has to score goals. His movement has a purpose, while that of the dancer has no other purpose than itself. Nevertheless, dance and soccer do have something in common: the training is hard. Even for Zidane. Because it has a religious meaning, grace is a dangerous word. You might think it is a gift, that you either have or you don't, and that there's nothing you can do to acquire it. But believe it or not, Zidane worked very hard to achieve his state of grace. He had certain facilities, he was gifted, yes—but work was what allowed him to realize himself. For Philippe Petit, it was the same. He is happy to admit it: "I don't have a net, but I've made a psychological net out of details." Before hurling himself into the void between the Twin Towers, he put in the hours. He thought of nothing else for months. Piece by piece, with the patience of a medieval craftsman, he constructed his mosaic, this perfect moment. For a few minutes of grace, he spent years in preparation. He warns: "It's a profession. Sober, harsh, deceptive. Anyone who isn't up for a long hard battle, with wasted effort, extreme dangers, and traps, who isn't prepared to sacrifice everything for the feeling of being alive, is not cut out to be a tightrope walker." And anyway, they wouldn't succeed. Does he have any tips? Simple: "Work, work, work. The wire has to gradually come to belong to you." Only then, "after long hours of training, will the moment come when all difficulty falls away. Everything is possible. Everything feels light." So, ease comes at the end. Not at the beginning. But after how many hours of training? "Don't expect to get anything from one serious session of a few hours," he warns. "It has to get under your skin." When, in the days of Edith Piaf, you said someone had got "under your skin," it meant there was nothing to be done, you had no choice: love is a yes or no affair, you can't change it, that's just how it is. Love at first sight is like friendship for Montaigne: "Because it was him, because it was me." Friend or lover, you've got them under your skin. Or not. Whereas soccer, tightrope walking, violin, piano, dance, all activities that depend on expert gestures, have to be literally "incorporated." Through toil, sweat, and time. Everyone knows work is necessary. You can't go directly from the square that says "couch" to the one that says "champ" just by throwing a dice or saying some magic words. Even to be able to do magic, you have to go to school—just ask Harry Potter. The goal of all work is to acquire a second nature, which in the end will allow you to accomplish with ease what is difficult at first. All facility comes from surmounting difficulty. As they say in the military: "tough training, easy war." There are no short-cuts. Isn't what we call talent, when examined closely, really work, more or less concealed? And when we speak of genius, isn't that really clandestine work? No one doubts the necessity for training, we can all agree about that—but the question is *how much*?

Remember Malcolm Gladwell? He's a writer at the *New Yorker*, and I love reading his books. In *Outliers*, which here is used to mean "exceptional successes," Gladwell gives a precise answer to that question "how many?" Ten thousand hours, according to him, is the "magic number of greatness." You want to become exceptional in any given domain? It's "easy": you just have to devote 10,000 hours to it, or ten years, to become an expert or perform at a high level. Strangely enough, this is exactly the conclusion Stendhal arrived at: "Write every day for an hour or two. Genius or not." Ten years of writing for one or two hours a day, somewhere between 3,652 and 7,304 (counting leap years) gets you close to 10,000 hours. You'd only need to write between two and three hours a day to get there. Stendhal seems to be saying, like Gladwell, that what we mistake for genius is simply the result of hard work; ten years' hard work, to be precise.

Why ten years, when by working ten hours a day you'd get to 10,000 hours in a thousand days, which is less than three years? Because it's not enough to accumulate hours of practice; the practice has to be *deliberate*, it has to represent an *effort* to achieve a specific goal, ability, or gesture that as yet eludes you. To put it another way, you need to feel the time passing, it needs to not be easy. This is quite different from the so-called ten hours a day spent by Zola or Flaubert, who seem like workaholics when in fact they spent most of their time dreaming of the right word, "fiddling around" with their sentences like Giacometti fiddling around with his clay; in short, doing what they liked best, which takes a lot of deliberately wasted time and a certain kind of nonchalance. Nothing to do with *continuous* effort, in any case. Three or four hours a day of deliberate practice, preferably spread out over several sessions, would therefore be a maximum, because the effort of all that attention is exhausting. The rest of the day should be spent resting, or in comparatively less intense activities: reading, reflection, strategy, associated leisure activities, and so on. Three to four hours a day with one day of rest a week, and two weeks of holiday a year, gets you to 1,000 hours a year, or 10,000 hours in ten years.

So it takes ten years to become an *outlier*. While we're on the subject, notice the contradiction between the title of the book and its content, since by definition it is impossible to generalize on the basis of special cases. Even if an exception does occasionally prove the rule, it's impossible to see how to establish any rule whatsoever on the basis of exceptions. But Gladwell proposes a "rule of 10,000 hours," illustrated by examples like the Beatles or Bill Gates. If you think they're geniuses, Gladwell explains, you're missing the key part of their story. Essentially, genius is a concept invented by the lazy. It allows one to think that successful people only had to get themselves born, while in fact circumstances gave them the chance to become exceptional by giving them the opportunity to work more than others. In the case of the Beatles, for example, Gladwell tells us how their manager decided, when they were still a band with very little experience, to send them to Hamburg to play several gigs a day in dodgy clubs for months on end. By Gladwell's analysis, what should have been an ordeal became an opportunity, increasing their experience and maturity, toughening them up and getting them to 10,000 hours while other bands who stayed in Liverpool or elsewhere in England only got to play for a few hours at the weekend. This competitive advantage gave them a head start of several lengths once they got back to England, and gave them their breakthrough. Bill Gates? Same phenomenon. At the time when he started to get interested in computers and programming, you had to wait a week to access the university's one computer for even a few minutes. But his mother, who worked in a hospital, arranged for him to have access, every evening, to the computer in her workplace, which no one used at night. Bill Gates took his chance and clocked up hours of experience every day—or, rather, every night. This was transformed into a huge competitive advantage for him a few years later, when he entered the race in the development of personal computers. So you thought the Beatles were the Rimbaud of pop and Bill Gates the Mozart of computer science? Well, you were wrong—they were simply serious workers, hardworking artisans, maybe inspired grafters, but above all, they put in the hours. Besides, Rimbaud, on closer examination, that so-called genius poet and author of the famous line "No one is serious when they're seventeen," was actually extremely serious, and won the general Latin verse prize when he was only fifteen years old. Rimbaud, the classic outcast poet, all of whose work was written before the age of twenty, was above all a star pupil, and excellent at Latin, which he wrote fluently, without the need for a dictionary. If you add up the writing of his poems, his study of Latin, and his advanced reading, it must easily come to 10,000 hours. What about Mozart? Initiated into the subtleties of the harpsichord by his father at the age of five, at fourteen he could transcribe Allegri's *Miserere*, a complex work that lasts a quarter of an hour, having only heard it once. Impressed? Add it up: by the age of fourteen Mozart had easily done his 10,000 hours, and more. Rimbaud and Mozart didn't come out of nowhere; they just started early.

Ten thousand hours in ten years, I hear you say, OK, that sounds pretty good, pretty serious without being impossible— but how did Malcolm Gladwell arrive at this exact, nice round number? It all comes from a 1993 study led by K. Anders Ericsson (at Florida State University) and two other psychologists at the world-renowned music academy of Berlin. I'll give you the gist: take thirty violin students, chosen by their teachers, and divided up into groups of ten in three categories: the "best," the future international solo artists; the "good," the future orchestral players; and the "less good," classed as "future music teachers" [sic]. They all devoted 50.6 hours a week to studying music, whether in the form of theory lessons, practical lessons, concerts, etc. Apparently they all spent the same amount of time working on their instruments, but with one key difference: the first two groups spent 24.3 hours a week on private practice, i.e., working alone, compared with only 9.3 hours for the last group. Another significant difference: the violinists in the first two groups reckoned they slept about sixty hours a week, compared with 54.6 in the last group. So, more personal work, and more rest. Up to this point, there was still no difference between the "best" and the "good." But when they were asked to estimate retrospectively how many hours of practice they had accumulated on the violin, it was then discovered that even if the first two groups did the same amount of weekly private practice, the best simply started younger. By the age of twelve, they already had 1,000 hours' lead on the future teachers. At eighteen, the future soloists had done on average 7,410 hours of private practice, the good players 5,310 hours, and the future teachers 3,420. "So there is a direct correlation," concluded the psychologists, "between the level of competence of the groups and the average total private practice time on the violin." Since we see similar results with pianists, the researchers estimate that expert musicians, whatever their instrument, have, on average, clocked up 10,000 hours of practice by the age of twenty. Or to put it more precisely, I should repeat that that means "purposeful practice," in which the players willingly apply themselves to difficult exercises that demand an effort, the kind of practice that by definition must be solitary, because it is high risk, and needs to be conducted away from the judgment of peers. In an article entitled "The Role of Deliberate Practice in the Acquisition of Expert Performance," Ericsson and his co-authors extended their conclusion to sport. In sport, as in music, what we assume is a gift, an innate talent, is in fact simply the result of years of serious training. Based on approximations and generalization, this study, carried out on violinists, would go on to become the "10,000-hour rule," according to which 10,000 hours are both necessary and sufficient to become an expert in any chosen field. The message is encouraging, democratic, and egalitarian, because it supposes that "you can if you want to," and that hard work will take you as far as you want to go. But it has also led to an increase in early training for children, in sport as in music, and confirms the prejudice that says that if you don't make progress in any given domain, it's because you haven't worked hard enough. The message both liberates (anything is possible) and blames (if you don't succeed it's all your own fault). The "magic number of greatness," as Gladwell calls it, can easily be used to stigmatize.

Dan McLaughlin, having read Gladwell, took this number seriously and decided, on April 5, 2010, the day he turned thirty, to drop everything and devote himself to golf with the aim of becoming a professional at the end of 10,000 hours. In order for the experiment to be convincing, he needed to have no particular physical gifts, and to have never played golf. This was indeed the case. He describes himself as a completely average person. If it worked for him, it would work for anyone. He started a blog and set his plan in motion. He consulted with Ericsson himself, who drew up a timetable for him, and he engaged a professional golf instructor. Six hours a day, six days a week. Or, rather, eight hours, because he spent two hours thinking and analyzing, to give himself a break. Six hours a day is practically twice the "normal" pace. At that rate he should have finished his 10,000 hours and become a professional by the end of 2016.

But it wasn't that simple. Even Ericsson acknowledged that his study involved too few subjects to be generalizable. In addition, they were subjects who had been both selected and trained. So it was impossible to differentiate between what was innate and what was acquired, what was due to talent and what was due to work. The study is constructed in such a way as to disregard anything that might come from natural talent. It is also a retrospective study, and the estimates given by the violinists varied by as much as 500 hours. Lastly, and most importantly, the 10,000 hours are only an *average*. On average, the best had worked for 10,000. But we don't know the variance—that is, the degree to which the different subjects in the study were adrift of the average.

David Epstein, in *The Sports Gene*, puts his finger on this detail (which is more than a mere detail), and suggests we consider chess. Chess is different from the violin. Since players are ranked according to a system of international points—"Elo points" (named after the system's creator)—one can know the exact level of a chess player, and follow their progression precisely. In 2007, psychologists Guillermo Campitelli and Fernand Gobet conducted a study of 104 players of different levels. An average player has around 1,200 Elo points. A master has between 2,200 and 2,400. A grand master has over 2,500. They saw that to reach the threshold of 2,200 points and become a professional took an average of 11,053 hours. A bit more than the 10,000 hours for musicians. Where it gets complicated is that according to individuals, the number of hours they have spent varies from 3,000 to 23,000. Twenty thousand hours' difference, or twenty years of "purposeful practice"! Some people need to train for eight times longer than others to reach the same level. There are also players who tot up 25,000 hours without reaching master level. And there is no guarantee they will *ever* reach it.

It's the same in sport. A study of triathletes shows that within the same level there are differences of a factor of ten. Some people had to train ten times more than others to reach the same standard. Moreover, with the same amount of training, we see what sociologists call the "Matthew effect," named after the Gospel According to St. Matthew, in which it is said that to those who have, more will be given, and from those who have nothing, the little they have will be taken away. This is not quite correct, because training works for everyone, but far from compensating for natural differences, it simply deepens them irretrievably. The best become better more quickly than the good, and the others don't even get a mention.

According to the rule of 10,000 hours, though, it's the number of hours spent training that should explain the variations. Now, according to another study (also conducted by Ericsson, this time with darts players rather than violinists), after fifteen years of practice, only 28 percent of the variation in performance can be attributed to training. To put it another way, you can train your whole life without ever catching up on the difference between yourself and the best, or acquiring real expertise. The rule of 10,000 hours, David Epstein concludes, with some humor, would be better called the rule of 10,000 years.

In any case, putting in your 10,000 hours in your given area absolutely does not guarantee that you will reach expert level. You need both the innate "hardware" (the "cables," the computer), which comes from nature, and the acquired "software," which comes from training. To achieve greatness there is no magic number of hours that will allow you to substitute work for being gifted. You need both: the gift and hard work. The gift without the work will go uncultivated, the work without the gift will be sterile. In both cases, it's a waste. It's a pity not to train if you're gifted, but training when you have no gift can be harmful. You may incur needless harm to your physique and to your ego, and tenacity or denial can turn into blindness and useless obstinacy.

Dan McLaughlin knows about this—he had to abandon his "Dan Plan" in 2015, following a back injury that forced him to interrupt his "purposeful practice," and in fact his practice altogether. Accident? Tiredness? Somatization? The 10,000 hours literally weighed him down. His body said "stop!" after 6,000 hours. After two years of silence and denial, when he was on the verge of depression, he wound up his experiment in 2017 with a last message on the site he'd set up in 2010 to keep a record of his progress:

> I apologize that this has taken me almost two years to write. It was never my desire to change directions and hang up the sticks. It was after having a heavy heart for a long time that I finally realized my own physical limitations and what I needed to do to move on in life. I did not even admit to myself that this was over until earlier this year and even then it seemed like I had not fully accepted the reality of it all. [...] I am not in any way happy to have had to hang up the clubs, but after having enough time to properly process every-

thing I have come to realize that some things are out of our hands and it's not about what you want to do in an ideal world, it's about what you do with the circumstances that are presented.

True courage, for him, turned out to be recognizing his limits and his humanity, and renouncing his desire to be all-powerful. He discovered the Stoics' precept that if we want to be happy, we need to focus on the things we can control, and leave the rest to the gods. In this sense his experiment taught him something, and his failure is a success, because he became aware of his own physical reality, and of reality itself. One point in his favor: it took only 6,000 hours for him to realize this and to become an expert in stoicism; that's 4,000 hours fewer than predicted. That's not counting the two years of doubt and denial, which makes 365 a 2 × 24 (since depression is twenty-four hours a day), equaling the 17,500 hours of "purposeful depression" that it took him to realize that the rule of 10,000 hours perhaps didn't exist or wasn't valid for him. The rule of 10,000 hours flatters us because it allows us to think that with enough work, we can become whatever we want. That everything depends on individual will and a sense of effort. If performance was only about training, if 10,000 hours really were sufficient to compensate for natural differences, why continue to separate men and women in competitions? Because, as David Epstein shows, just because we want to doesn't mean we can. To think you didn't become a golf champion after 10,000 hours because you didn't work hard enough is as misguided as to believe that a champion doesn't need to train, that they just have to exist to win. The temptation of 10,000 hours, for all its whiff of egalitarianism, offers an even more dangerous illusion than the inverse temptation to just let it all hang out. You can't afford to skimp on training, nor to underestimate your limits. We shouldn't say "if you want to, you can" but "if you can, you're right to want it."

Now it's true that Zinedine Zidane was only twenty-six years old when he headed the ball into the goal twice in the 1998 World Cup Final against Brazil. Since he started out at AS Cannes at fourteen, he must have easily done his 10,000 hours. And the training sessions at Juventus, in Turin, where he continued his development in 1998, are famously tough. Zinedine had to sweat blood to become Zidane. And Philippe Petit, when he stepped out between the Twin Towers in 1974, was just short of his twenty-fifth birthday. Since the moment he started training, he must have clocked up more than 10,000 hours. And he had experience of great heights: in 1971 he'd walked on a rope between the towers of Notre-Dame. In 1973 he had done the same thing between the pylons of the Sydney Harbour Bridge, the widest bridge in the world.

But let's ask ourselves simply and honestly: if you really think about it, who actually believes, without doubting the virtue of trying, that with 10,000 hours they could, if not become world champion, then at least reach the top level in their discipline of choice? For anyone who's hesitating about the answer, here's another question, which we should all be able to agree on: Who thinks that 10,000 hours of training would give them the courage to walk on a wire 400 meters off the ground? Or, more modestly, just to start small, between the towers of Notre-Dame?

4

The Experience of Grace

The divine is effortless

AESCHYLUS

Yannick Noah loves music. Singing gets him high. Dancing is pure pleasure. One day, he promises, he'll make it his career. For now, he's a professional tennis player. He hasn't won the French Open yet. It's December 12, 1982, 7 in the morning in a Toulouse nightclub, and he's giving it all he's got on the dance floor, drunk as a skunk, with a group of friends. It's party time. Except that in a few hours, six, to be precise, he has to play in a final against the Czech, Tomáš Šmíd, at 1 p.m. on the dot. This is what happens when your friends suggest just popping out for one drink, and you can't say no. When the club closes, it's bright daylight. For reasons not clear to him, he undresses, throws his clothes into the astonished market crowd, rolls around in the gutter, and goes back to the hotel in his underpants. By the time he finally shuts his eyes it's already time to open them again (you will be familiar with that feeling that you've slept for only a minute even though your watch might say something different). It's ten minutes past midday. Black coffee, croissants, aspirin, Alka Seltzer. Soon after, he appears on court. And contrary to all expectations, particularly his own, he wins 6-3, 6-2, while in a complete trance.

What happened? What can we learn from this story? Firstly: sport doesn't always have a moral, but it does have its own logic. Hangovers are not recommended as training or preparation for top-level competition, but on this occasion, it worked: instead of brooding alone in his room, thinking about the next day's match and ending up with insomnia, by partying through the night Yannick succeeded in forgetting what was at stake. With his brain cleared of all worry, the athlete, more rested than he thinks, can play in a state of complete relaxation because he has no expectations. His relative indifference to the outcome means he can trust his body completely and experiment with letting go, that so-called miracle remedy for the stress of modern life, which usually eludes us in direct proportion to the degree to which we seek it out. This is to be expected: if I say "let go!" you will focus on doing so, and become tense. Like a snake consuming its own tail, it's impossible to let go if that's all you're thinking about. Whereas thanks to the alcohol, his body was on autopilot, without being hindered, or only very slightly, by consciousness. A form of self-forgetting, of non-thinking, a kind of spontaneous Zen state in which one succeeds at everything, because one has ceased to aim for anything. Relaxation is a precondition for such a state. One must trust one's own body completely, and put it in charge of the controls. And if it sounds a bit like being drunk, yes, it is! Don't tell anyone, but all the signs suggest that a sleepless night with lots of booze is the closest you can get to a state of grace. Tightrope walker Philippe Petit admits to having had the same experience as Yannick Noah: "Drunk with alcohol, I have proved that a body that knows what it is doing does not need a mind to lead it." The way the body—the expert—steers itself when in a state of inebriation, or, rather, the way it acts on autopilot, when we've given it permission to steer itself, is not an exemplary method, but I mention it here by way of proof. It is proof that it is possible to let the body do its own thing, when it *knows*. If it knows, you'll say, it must be because it's learned, irrespective of how many hours it's done. Tightrope walker and tennis player alike, for you to trust your body to the point of allowing it to do its thing, it has to have been trained. It's not just about the number of hours spent, as we saw in the last chapter. Then what is it about?

The next year, in 1983, this time sober and well prepared, Yannick Noah won the French Open. As he scored the match point he felt light: "My feet are off the ground, I'm flying, I'm lighter than air. Like in a dream? No, not even that, it's like ... well, like nothing else." It's a feeling he would only ever have once again, a few years later, one morning in bed, only half awake: pure, unadulterated happiness: "From the tips of my fingers to the ends of my hair, I *am* happiness. Nothing can touch me. Twenty seconds. I can't see him, but I sense the presence of my grandfather." A grandfather who is no longer of this world, but who appears in it. A mystical but above all a physical experience. An experience, sadly, that never seems to last very long. But when you've known happiness like that, you can never forget it. You just hope for one thing: that you'll find it again.

*

Zinedine Zidane might say the same thing about the World Cup in 2006. He had left the French team in 2004, but suddenly decided to come back for a grand finale, after a late-night conversation, as in a dream, with a mysterious stranger who persuaded him to don the blue shirt one more time. He won't say more than that about it but this admission is extraordinary from such a famously reserved player. It was to be both a comeback and a final farewell: "For me it was everything, I put everything into it, everything I had inside, right to the core." And the man they said was too old, that some had said was finished, the man for whom every match might have been his last, was better than he'd ever been. Spain and Portugal would pay the price. But, as in 1998, he played his greatest match against Brazil, this time in the quarter final, on July 1, 2006, in Frankfurt. A perfect match, from start to finish. Every time he touched the ball there was magic. Jean-Michel Larqué, a former international player himself, and legendary commentator for the French national team, known for his sharp tongue, still raves about it: "I've never seen a player do that on the pitch. A work of art." Zidane keeps it more prosaic: "We got into the match straight away...We were facing Brazil, so what the hell—if we lose we lose." Paradoxically, because the Brazilians are so good, it's easy to play against them: there's absolutely nothing to lose. Even less in 2006 than back in 1998, because it wasn't even the final. The atmosphere between the two teams in the corridor from the dressing rooms to the pitch was genuinely relaxed; there was laughter, hugging—they were just happy to be playing together. Sometimes you play against someone, but this time they were playing with. Brazil was an opponent unlike any other; it would have been every soccer player's dream to play them. No pressure, just pleasure. And you could feel it: "We were really into the match, properly into it. We had that feeling you get, that at this point nothing could go wrong. You're just out there having a great time, enjoying yourself. Especially when we scored. When we scored we felt like we were on cloud nine."

Bixente Lizarazu confirms this: "He was just like an angel in that match, I've never seen anything like it. You felt he wasn't human." Zidane is modest, but also knows he was exceptional that day: "What can I say? It's subjective, it's always subjective when people say I did things that were somehow different.

They said the real Brazilian out there that evening was Zidane. All I know is that if I'd been out there alone I'd have done nothing." It was all down to team spirit, and perhaps just spirit. A sense of invulnerability, perfection, eternity, of being outside of normal time: "We were in the dressing room, we were like, OK, what the heck, we wanted to go on playing, it was just so great. It was *so* great. It was..." Zidane smiles, lost in memories. That day, for the first and last time in his career, he danced naked, up on the physio's table. There are no words. Yannick Noah, who watched the match, like everyone else, tries to find some:

> He was in a state of grace. I've tried to find that state, I've worked on it, I try to transmit it, to dissect it. There are days when all of a sudden you've got all the elements in place and it comes naturally, because you've been working at it for fifteen years, and suddenly for no obvious reason, you're touched by grace. I remember various moves he made, I remember them winning, of course, but mostly his moves, and especially his face. His face, look, even while I'm telling you this, I've got goosebumps, it was just so extraordinary. And the way he just kept looking up at the sky. You know, it was...

Noah is lost in the deliciousness of the memory too, and his conclusion is the same as Zidane's: there just aren't any words; "those moments really are rare."

Once his playing career was over, Yannick Noah became the

captain of the French Davis Cup team, which won in 1991, 1996, and, after a big gap, 2017. Since he's been training other players, he has continued to refine his thoughts on the conditions required for surpassing oneself, individually or in a group. He doesn't like to talk about a state of grace, even if he did when talking about Zidane. "It's a beautiful expression, but the problem with it is that it implies that the person in that state has no real control over what's happening. When in fact it's the exact opposite." So he prefers the expression "in the zone," which implies, contrary to the state of grace, a total mastery of the situation. Someone "in the zone" plays to perfection without needing to think about it; everything becomes instinctive, natural, easy. It has all the advantages of being drunk, without the hangover. You can enter and leave the zone by chance, but the aim is to be able to enter it at will. Grace is something you receive, the religious origins of the term suggesting a kind of passivity or prayer; the zone is something you conquer, it's a word synonymous with activity and industry, and also territory, which can be occupied. Grace is a state, while a zone is a space. Etymologically, "zone" comes from the Greek for "belt" or "girdle." Personally, I prefer to talk about a "point of action," the point where you meet with yourself, where you've eliminated the gap between intention and action. The point of action is a natural point, where you no longer need to think about what you are going to do, because you're already doing it. It's the point where you are both the most at ease and the most active, a point of concentration and forgetfulness, where you are most yourself because you're no longer thinking about yourself. Where everything you do is true to yourself and is in tune with your idea of life. It's the point where everything comes together and makes sense. A point of concentration, where your relationship with yourself and with others and the world is harmonious. It's a happy point, is my point.

It doesn't matter whether you like or loathe sport, practice it or not: the question of ease or grace touches everyone, and all areas of life. Sport is our example here because it is particularly easy to understand. It's easy to see when someone isn't "in their body," or the opposite, when someone *is* "in the game" or "in the race." Françoise Sagan, describing her own point of action, her moments of grace in writing, also used a sporting metaphor:

> when it "takes off" it's like a well-oiled machine that functions to perfection. It's like when you see someone run one hundred meters in ten seconds. You see the miracle of sentences mounting up, and your mind functions almost outside itself. You become a spectator of yourself. When that happens, I write really easily, and I just can't stop. And when it works it's fantastic. They're really blessed moments. Yes, sometimes, you feel just like the queen of words. It's extraordinary, it's paradise. When you believe in what you're writing it's an incredible pleasure. You feel like queen of all the earth.

For pianist Hélène Grimaud, who is as famous for her conservation work with wolves as for the beauty of her playing, the artist at the keyboard is in a state of "visitation." They "vibrate" with the intuition of a presence, their "thought suddenly receives a kind of illumination, and in turns moves the body accordingly." Here the vocabulary is no longer that of the sports field; it's both religious and supernatural.

> Through hard work, the pianist prepares for the moment of visitation. As I walk across the stage, I'm alone, and the moment I start playing, I cease to be. A presence is protecting me. Is it the presence of the music? Of the composers whose work I'm playing? It's as though there are two of me and I can watch myself playing at the same time as continuing to play—sometimes I see a light come down that casts a halo around the piano and I know that that light is them.

This "being two of me" is similar to what Françoise Sagan refers to when she talks about the "miracle" you see happen as though you were a "spectator" or in "paradise," a state in which you function "almost outside yourself." Hélène Grimaud dispenses even with the "almost"—not her style—and describes an experience that is both mystical and physical—as you might expect of a true mystic. She becomes, she says, "a witch, a medium," and summons the spirits of composers as she plays their music. You may smile—or shudder—at this. Or simply admire the fact that a professional pianist should not be content simply with performing the music but seeks to experience it in a prophetic state. One may also receive illumination without already being enlightened, and Hélène Grimaud is able also to explain the nature of this illumination, to describe it analytically. The experience of grace is, in the first instance, an alteration of one's relationship with time: each time the pianist "turns a page, they are also turning time, as the future rises to meet them, rather than their being borne toward it." When you perform a score you're traveling in time, or rather watching time travel toward you. The pianist "gathers everything in an endless present; at the very end she rises, in rapture: the ground vanishes into the distance below her fingers." The present may be without limits, but it is natural that it should also meet the past, and allow one to come into contact with the composer, who has had similar experiences. Through playing a piece by a composer, you feel what they felt, live what they lived, you feel their presence in their work. Hélène Grimaud says she is particularly sensitive to Robert Schumann; the moment she discovered his music she felt as if she knew him. Nothing surprising there, really: artists are all in some sense mediums, who can communicate beyond space and time with each of us, through their works. Everyone's had the feeling that a book, a film, or a piece of music was made for them. Artists are our soul mates, who look for moments of grace in order to share them with us. The paradox is that in that state of grace, we are so "inside it" that nothing else exists, there's nothing to share: "There are moments," Schumann writes, "when music completely possesses me, when sounds are all there are, to precisely the point where it's impossible for me to transcribe anything at all." When "it works," it's impossible to stop what you're doing and take notes. Similarly, when it's not going well, there's not much you can do about it: "Piano went very badly yesterday, as though someone was holding back my arm. I didn't want to force it. Doubt and darkness seemed to cover all people here below, and the skies above." Robert Schumann and Hélène Grimaud both know there's no point in forcing it. You must prepare for the visitation, but hard work is no guarantee that illumination will come. Work is just the anteroom of grace.

So grace is never guaranteed, and the very best, like the rest of us, are reduced just to hoping. But to know this kind of grace, to feel yourself king or queen of the earth, you don't need to be a champion of anything: soccer, tennis, literature, or music simply serve here to underline the oneness of the experience, of the point of action, when "it takes," when "it works," when it's "just great," when "it" is impossible to express in words or transcribe with notes, because talking, like composing, means detaching yourself from what you're experiencing, coming out of it and commenting on it, instead of staying "in it." The best way of talking about the point of action, then, is through the *dot dot dot* of an ellipsis...

But how do you reach that point? If you've already experienced the "zone" or "grace" or "the point of action," the best way to get back to it is to reconstitute the route by which you got there. Yannick Noah calls that "Tom Thumb's pebbles." What were you doing in the hours leading up to it? What environment were you in? Which objects, which people did you have around you? What were you thinking about? Relax, just let those memories and those feelings come. Take note of everything, mentally, or in writing. For example, for Françoise Sagan, who answered many questions from journalists on this subject, it might work something like this:

I work at night, because it's the only time when you can get on with your work in peace, without the phone ringing, or people dropping by...without being disturbed. Working at night in Paris is like working in the country. A dream! I work from midnight till six in the morning. Daytime is monstrous, constant meetings. Nighttime is like a smooth sea, it's endless. I like to see the sun come up before I go to bed. I can write a novel over several periods of ten to fifteen days. In between, I think about the story, I daydream, and I talk about it. Some ideas I lose. In the country, I work in the afternoon. The good thing about the country is being able to get up and go for a wander outside, look at the grass, the weather that day. In the afternoon, around 4 o'clock, you say to other people: "I have to go and work now." You complain, you groan, you put on a little act. And what is so charming is that when it's gone well with your typewriter or your pen, you forget it's time to eat. That's not to say I work better in the country. I can work pretty well anywhere: on a bench, under a tree, I'm a bit like a pregnant woman. She doesn't think about her child all the time, but every now and then she feels a kick that reminds her it's there. [Sometimes] it's in the middle of the night. I switch the light on, I look everywhere for a pencil, I note down my idea on a piece of paper and the next day I've lost it. I make lots of notes, but only to do with ideas. It's important to be lazy. Books are made to a large extent out of wasted time, daydreaming, thinking about nothing.

Yannick Noah wrote a whole book about the question of whether a method exists for "getting into the zone," and if it can be applied to the whole of one's life: *Secrets, etc* . . . (notice the ellipsis in the title). Without giving away those "secrets," we can touch on a few of them here, the first one being perhaps the most important: "In 1991," he writes, "when I decided to draw my career to a close, the discovery of yoga fundamentally transformed my perception of life. I realize that I could have played tennis for pleasure and relaxation, but as I wasn't familiar with those concepts, I played forcefully, ferociously." Ironically it was just when he stopped playing that Yannick Noah discovered the virtues of gentleness and letting go. The first condition of the appearance of grace is not trying to force it. Yannick Noah's situation is quite unique: as a player, he only ever really experienced grace once, at the French Open in 1983, and ever since he has been trying to work out what he was missing in the following years, so he might repeat his success. Grace eludes whoever seeks it "ferociously," but once he gave up playing, Noah finally understood it and tried to share it with others.

Zinedine Zidane also wonders about the origin of the grace people associate him with. Of course, he doesn't use this word. He is suspicious of it. And rightly so. He knows better than anyone how hard he worked, he knows what sacrifices he made, from a very early age, to reach the highest level. But he also knows, because he experienced it several times over, that there is something higher than the highest level, something or someone even higher, that has the last word in this story, in *his* story. Why, for example, in the 1998 World Cup, having not scored a goal in the whole competition, did he suddenly wake up and reveal himself in the final, scoring two goals, one after the other, against Brazil? When it really counts—in fact, when it counts double? Two headers, even, when he would be the first to admit that they're not his forte. Or to give another example: how, in the 2002 Champions League Final, did he find the nerve to hit the ball on the volley and send it into the net? A perfect gesture, supernatural in its clarity, as though his body was simply taking orders. Zidane says, in a documentary justly titled *Zidane, un destin d'exception* (Zidane: An Exceptional Destiny): "It's one of those things that happens once in a lifetime. OK, so it happened to me. Afterward you wonder about it, you say: 'Did someone help me or didn't they?' At any rate, I always say...someone's looking out for me…" Who is that "someone" that might be helping? Is Zidane religious? He doesn't say. But in saying this he admits that he feels someone's with him, protecting him with a supernatural power, or at the least, a lucky star.

When you watch Zidane execute what is considered one of the most beautiful goals in the history of the European Cup, you get the feeling it's easy for him, that he just had to want it, and it happened. You know, even as you watch, that you would be incapable of doing the same thing. But where it gets interesting is that Zidane feels exactly the same. That gesture, which no one could have predicted, is impossible to reproduce, even for him. He says quite calmly that he has never managed to reproduce in training what he managed to do without thinking in that final. The important words here are "without thinking." It was an "uncontrolled" kick. By not thinking about it, Zidane succeeded. Or to put it more precisely: he succeeded because he didn't think about it *and* because he's Zidane. Not thinking about it won't make you play like him. That would be too easy. But when you're Zidane, there comes a moment when you don't need to think anymore, when it's much better not to. When soccer has become second nature to you, an instinct, and when your body just knows—then you have to let it get on with it.

What's most remarkable in what he does here is not so much the actual move as that he dared attempt it at such a moment. It wasn't just the final, it was a final that Zidane had already lost twice, in 1997 and 1998, while playing for Juventus. His greatest fear was that he'd lose again, this time playing for Real Madrid, and become, in the eyes of his teammates, of the soccer world, of everyone, the "black cat" who puts a jinx on things. Zidane's greatest achievement, in this match where the stakes were so incredibly high, was not allowing this thinking to paralyze him. How did he manage this? He doesn't describe his method, and I'm not sure he actually had one, but he can describe his mental process at the moment when, four years later, in 2006, in the World Cup Final against Italy, he had to take a penalty after only seven minutes played, against Buffon, a legendary goalkeeper who knew him like the back of his hand, having faced him many times during Zidane's years playing for Juventus. Taking a penalty is a mental test like no other, especially for such a great player, who has everything to lose. Missing a penalty in the World Cup Final would mark him forever, particularly as this was the last match of his career. When you take a penalty, irresolution is the worst of all evils, as Descartes said, several centuries before soccer was invented. As Zidane himself explains, the penalty is a particular move. Since it isn't a piece of action within the game, and you do prepare for it, there's no way you can rely on instinct: "It's better to know in advance where you're going to put it, because you may get a surprise." You have to decide before you start moving, choose a side, how hard you're going to kick it, how high, and not change your mind in midstream. The slightest doubt, the slightest hesitation, due, for example, to a movement by the goalie, and you'll immediately suffer for it. As Zidane moved forward to shoot, the whole world held its breath. Usually he shoots with the inside of his right foot and crosses the ball into the left-hand corner of the net. Against all expectation, all logic, and all caution, Zidane permitted himself to do something crazy: a Panenka (named after its inventor). He shot at the center of the goal, straight at the goalie, but with no great effort, just jabbing at the ball so that it dropped in like a dead leaf. He was counting on Buffon anticipating, and in fact Buffon had already set off to the right, where he knew Zidane usually placed it. Wrong-footed, the Italian goalkeeper had time to stop his movement and turn around, to see the ball bounce behind his goal line after hitting the crossbar. It was a bit like if a tennis player on match point attempted an unlikely drop shot on the line, instead of the easy, expected, smash. Yannick Noah is admiring: "Just when millions of others would have been terrified and gone for the safe option, he decides to play around. Incredible, isn't it?" Incredible but true. Why do something so risky, in the World Cup Final, with millions of people watching? According to him, even the man himself has no idea. Zidane: "It's actually something instantaneous. I think... Between the moment when I put the ball down, I take my run-up, I'm about to shoot, it's then, that's when it happens. Not even before that. It happens then, in those ten seconds. I say, OK, that's what I've got to do." Apparently Zidane, against his own recommendation, did not know what he was going to do before he did it. It just happened. But if you listen very carefully, in the moment just before he kicked, he did know. Zidane confirms Descartes' second maxim: in order to make a good decision you don't need to think about it for long, or even think about it at all. You just have to make it and stick with it. In this case it was instant. It coincided as far as was possible with the execution. No place for doubt. No time, quite simply. It goes so fast that it's hard to tell if Zidane made the decision or the decision made Zidane. This immediateness, this instantaneousness, is a condition for success. So Zidane does have a method: even if the penalty can't be an instinctive gesture, in this case he managed to make it as instinctive as possible, by thinking about it for as little time as possible. He managed both not to think about it and to make a decision. There is a kind of blindness or inspiration—it comes to the same thing—that allows you to risk the impossible, and pull it off. There's something impersonal too. When you find yourself at the point of action, it's as if you were no one, as if nothing, not even your own mind, can stand in the way of what the moment dictates. The point of action is also a point of inaction. When Zidane says "people are watching me," he's admitting he doesn't feel as though he has much say in what he does. He just knows he has to do it. As though it had been decreed, and he was simply carrying out his destiny. At the same time he recognizes a kind of premeditation in his move: "It had to be memorable." For his last match, precisely because it was a World Cup Final and everyone was watching, Zidane wanted to leave his mark. It couldn't be a penalty like any other. When Noah admires the fact that Zidane wasn't paralyzed by what was at stake, and just gave himself permission to "play," he's missing a vital element: what was really at stake, for Zidane, wasn't just winning the World Cup a second time, but winning it his way, his exceptional way, so he would go down in history once and for all.

*

The idea of destiny is often taken as a reason not to try. If everything has been foretold, you might be tempted to put your faith in higher powers and no longer take an active part in your own life: give up wanting, or trying, and quit the game. But destiny, if we understand it properly, is not a defeating but a liberating force. If everything's already been decided, then why worry about it? You might as well just play all out. You just have to be as fully yourself as possible, disregarding what's at stake. Far from being condemned to our destiny, we get the chance to be ourselves. It's our destiny after all. The idea of destiny is an invitation not to renounce, but to ease up. And that easing up, Noah explains, lets you play the very best game you can. Once you've rid yourself of the responsibility and the fear of doing badly, of "playing it safe," good-bye fear of winning, and farewell fear of losing. At last, just the pure joy of playing. For nothing; for pleasure.

Yannick Noah believes in destiny, as other people believe in a god. Faith, whatever its object, frees the body from thought. Nothing is more useful to someone undertaking something difficult than believing that somewhere it is already accomplished. Perhaps this is the reason why boxers, particularly heavyweights, the most dangerous, seem to have such great religious fervor. No one can forget Muhammad Ali, originally Cassius Clay, who converted to Islam. Certainly not George Foreman, his famous challenger in the "fight of the century," the Rumble in the Jungle in Kinshasa in 1974, who at the end of his career became a pastor in Texas. There is no doubt that believing in a god, any god, helps you get through difficult experiences and stand firm when the blows come crashing down. We suffer less when we believe our suffering has meaning. We feel less afraid if we know that God is watching over us. Philippe Petit, taking his first step out on the wire, is also doing something very close to religious faith. But if he does utter a prayer, it's to the gods in his feet and his legs, the gods his life depends on, and who, thanks to faultless preparation, chose to take up residence in his body. When Philippe Petit was arrested in the biggest cathedral in the world, St. John the Divine in New York, for having performed an illegal tightrope walk (as he had already done at Notre-Dame), James Parks Morton, the dean, immediately asked the police to release him. Far from being an intruder, he explained, the tightrope walker belonged to his cathedral:

> High-wire walking and cathedrals are sort of two sides of the same coin. It's a tradition. All you have to do is look in medieval manuscripts and you see towers and you see wire walkers. It's one of these tremendous moments in which

everything is in the balance. It's life and death and it's heaven and hell. So it's a great offering. A cathedral is stone but a wire walker is a cathedral in motion.

When asked what he thought about the fact that Philippe Petit wasn't a believer, he replied wittily: "He doesn't need to believe in God, God believes in him."

5

Find the Right Position

Life is what I'm looking for, always

AUGUSTE RODIN

Ease is not an idea, it's a position. Sometimes it takes only the slightest adjustment, one small change, to feel comfortable in your armchair. It's important, so you need to take your time. Posture makes a big difference. You're not obeying some school or parental rule such as "Sit up properly!" or "Sit up straight!"—you're just finding the position in which you feel most at ease. Everything comes from that.

Before you can act you have to be "on receive." Not as an armchair passively receives your body, but more like an antenna receiving radio waves. It's up to you to position the antenna, to pick up clearly what's out there. Because everything is already out there, within reach. Whatever your situation, this is the first thing to get right: the position of your antenna, your position in the armchair. There's nothing you actually have to *do*; just allow the position to take shape by itself. The right position can only come from you, from your body, and not from a command or an order. Either it will come easily or it won't come at all. One thing is certain: no one will be able to force you into it. So take your time.

If you opened this book hoping to find a way of making your life easier, start by realizing that dream right now. Trust your body. Let it do its thing. Let yourself go. This is how all real change comes about. To escape difficulty, you need to stop resisting. Ease will come once you give it a chance.

Even in martial arts—especially in martial arts—your position comes first. That's the first thing you learn. If your posture is good, your breath comes more easily. Your joints won't hurt, your energy circulates: the state of rest is already an action. When I talked about the subject of this book to my friend Alexis, a mathematician specializing in time, who practices yoga and tai chi, he immediately started talking about François Roustang, an unusual psychoanalyst. A pupil of Lacan, over the course of a few years he went from traditional analysis based on language to using hypnosis as a therapeutic method. Not hypnosis like in films, where the subject is the victim of manipulation of which they are unconscious and which they can't remember afterward. No. Hypnosis is just suggestion, which one is free to follow or not. As when someone suggests: "Allow yourself to be put in the position that suits you," rather than "Put yourself...," which feels too violent and limiting. It's equally nothing to do with the aggressive strategy of aversion therapy, where you oblige someone to adopt precisely the behavior that frightens them, supposedly with a view to liberating them from it. As though it were enough to relive one's fear in order to make it disappear, as if fear could be worn out by being felt, when most of the time the feeling increases it, confirms it, anchors it deep inside you, and even makes it permanent in its intensified form: the fear of fear. We are afraid of being afraid, and justifiably, because once we fear it, we're already deep in it, with no way out. But how could you not anticipate fearfully the trial that is supposed to free you from fear? Fear always precedes its object. Hubert Grenier, my philosophy teacher in Louis le Grand lycée, would use the example of the Place de L'Étoile in Paris, for car drivers. Here, twelve straight avenues converge on one huge roundabout, where lanes are meaningless, and cars circle the Arc de Triomphe in an endless rush, often five-deep. It is so notoriously dangerous that rental companies offer two sets of car insurance for Paris: one including the Place de L'Étoile and the other excluding it. It can be terrifying. In this, as in many things, we feel the fear in advance, *when we think about it*. Whereas once we're out there, we just do the best we can. We are delivered from fear by action. This is why there is no need, for example, to force yourself to go up in a plane or into a flight simulator if you're afraid of flying, or to jump into a swimming pool if you're frightened of water. Repeating the trial over and over is not going to resolve the phobia. All you need to do for this, François Roustang says, right here and now, in your armchair, is adopt a desirable position. And the only desirable position is the one that brings you comfort. Careful now—relaxation is necessary for comfort, but true comfort isn't limited to relaxation:

> a comfortable position is one in which you are not just re-laxed, but in which all your limbs and your organs are mobi-lized. You need to feel that all your articulations are supple, and that energy is circulating in a constant flow, like a breath of wind passing from your head to your feet and from your feet up to your head.

Philosopher Michel Serres has coined a beautiful expression: to describe the body of the tennis player leaping for a volley or the goalkeeper waiting for a penalty, he speaks of the "possible body." Of course, the body is always the most real thing there is. But if the body manages to remain open to every eventuality, in other words, to anticipate nothing so as to be able to adapt to what happens, the body becomes "possible," ready for any-thing. It arranges itself as openly as possible, without allowing thought to interfere with feeling. Relaxation is not the opposite of action; it is the requirement for its being possible. If you wish to act, you have to be capable of a state of complete relaxation, from which action can burst like a thunderbolt. Relaxation, oddly, when you think about it, functions here like a spring. The greater the relaxation, the more concentrated and intense will be the action. Relaxation, in fact, allows energy to build up and circulate. What cures phobias is comfort, not suffering. The body, far from being made listless by comfort, on the contrary becomes available, ready for nothing in particular, and thus ready for anything. When your body is calm, your energy "circulates uninterrupted, like breath." This is an obvious first point, but sounds somehow surprising or paradoxical: a relaxed body has more energy than a tense one.

Before going any further, a quick question: how do you picture energy? What image does it conjure up? When you think of energy do you see a large muscle straining with effort, like the biceps of a bodybuilder or a heavyweight boxer, or do you see the slender silhouette and fluid movement of a long-distance runner? To help you choose, I suggest we visit the private collection of Auguste Rodin, in his company. The piece he is most proud of is a Greek statue of Hercules, hero of legendary strength, who triumphed in the famous twelve labors. How do you imagine it? If you see a superhero with massive muscles, huge arms, giant thighs, and big pecs, like a lifeguard in *Baywatch*, you're on the wrong track. "It is a statue," says art critic Paul Gsell, "that looks nothing like the great *Farnese Hercules*. It is wonderfully elegant. The torso and limbs of the demi-god, in all the pride of his youth, have an *extreme finesse*." Rodin's Hercules's strength is not massive, but light and lithe, his force slender. He has the frame of a long-distance runner, not of a sprinter on steroids. How else could he have outrun the deer with bronze hooves? The impression of robustness given by his body comes not from overblown muscles but from the harmony of its proportions. "Strength is often allied with grace," Rodin remarks, "and true grace is strong."

It took Rodin a while to understand this paradox. When he was young he confused strength with effort. "I reached the age of thirty-five without daring to abandon this false way of working as a sculptor. I always wanted to make strong, powerful things, but whatever I did, they looked small and lifeless. I knew it, but I couldn't help it. And even though I continued to work in this way I felt it wasn't right." In late 1875, having been stuck for months on a sculpture that would later be called *The Age of Bronze*, which he was desperately trying to rescue from failure, he suddenly decided to set off, at first on foot, then by train, for Italy, to see Michelangelo. Just a few days in Rome and Florence turned his life around and freed him from academicism. The very thing that Rodin had been searching for in vain for years by following the artificial rules of the Academy suddenly became clear to him when he beheld the naturalness of Michelangelo's statues. The evidence was right there before his eyes, the idea that all one has to do is follow nature, and it's easy; but he needed to go to Rome in order to discover what he could have found at home, or anywhere else.

A few years later, by now a teacher himself, Rodin—while in no way revoking his admiration for Michelangelo as a sculptor—expressed profound reservations regarding the meaning of his art. As we'll see, it's all about the position of the body. If you take a Greek marble, a Phidias, for example, you will notice that everything about it is harmonious, very supple, that the body is stripped of all effort, balanced, at rest. We can observe four directions in the sculpture,

> which produce a very gentle wave throughout the body. And this impression of tranquil charm is also created by the verticality of the body itself. The vertical line passing through the middle of the back of the neck arrives at the inner ankle bone of the left foot, which bears the entire weight of the body. In contrast, the other leg is free: it only touches the ground at the utmost tip of the toes, thus merely providing a second point of support: if necessary it could be lifted without the balance of the whole being disturbed.

It is a "posture full of abandon and grace. The way the sway of the shoulders is mirrored in the sway of the hips further adds to the serene elegance of the whole." To truly grasp what Rodin is saying here, I suggest you take up the posture of a Greek statue for a moment. Stand up. Put the whole weight of your body on your left leg, and place the right leg in front of you, touching the ground with the tip of your foot. Place one hand on your hip, let the other arm hang down, and your head should tilt naturally to one side. Your chest should be open, turned outward, convex, receiving the full force of the light. This position of rest, both nonchalant and attentive, sums up all the art of antiquity, which comes down to "joy in life, quietude, grace, balance, reason."

Now let's go over to the dark side. I suggest you adopt a

"Michelangelo" position. Remain seated. Turn your legs to one side, keeping them squeezed together, and turn your upper chest the other way. Bend your torso forward as though you're going to pick something up. Bend and press one arm against your body and bring the other behind your head. If you can see yourself in a mirror without having to twist any further, your attitude should express both extreme strength and "a strange sense of effort and torture." If we look at the perpendicular, "here it falls not onto one foot, but between the two: thus the two legs support the torso with what appears to be an effort." Instead of four planes there are now only two, one for the top of the body, the other going in the opposite direction, for the lower part.

> This lends the pose a feeling of both violence and constraint and provides an arresting contrast to the calm of antiquity. Both legs are folded, yet rather than being at rest, the two lower limbs seem to be working. The concentration of effort presses the two legs together and the two arms in against the body and the head. Thus all the space between the limbs and the trunk disappears: there are none of those openings which lightened Greek sculpture, created by the free disposition of the arms and legs: the art of Michelangelo creates statues in a single block.

Furthermore, your position is shaped like an S, typical of all statues of the Middle Ages, an attitude suggesting effort and melancholy, expressing suffering and disgust with life. This shape, "the console," "is the Virgin, seated, leaning in toward her child. It's the Christ nailed to the cross, his legs buckling, torso hanging toward mankind, whom his suffering must redeem. It's the *mater dolorosa* crouched over the body of her son." The concave torso, arched forward, where in classical art it was arched backward, produces very sharp shadows in the hollows of the chest and under the legs. "In short," says Rodin, "the most powerful genius of the modern age celebrated the epoch of shadows, while the Ancients sang of the epoch of light. His statues express the painful folding-in of a being on themselves, an anxious energy, the will to act with no hope of success, the suffering of the creature tormented by unrealizable aspirations." Michelangelo is the last and greatest gothic artist, appallingly tortured by melancholy. His favorite themes are the ones Rodin mentions: "the depth of the human soul, the holiness of effort and of suffering. [They] have an austere grandeur. But I cannot approve of his scorn for life. For my own part, I try constantly to make my vision of nature calmer. We should always tend toward serenity. There's no danger of our ever losing our Christian anxiety before mystery." Rodin distinctly prefers the sunny genius of Greek art to the tortured genius of Michelangelo.

You can trust in a sculptor: there is nothing more important than the position of the body. Depending on whether you start from grace or from effort, you will go either toward life or against it. If you want to try for a personal synthesis of grace and effort, just look at the example of the *Venus de Milo*, "marvel of marvels!," according to Rodin:

an exquisite rhythm, but beyond that, a pensive quality; for here we no longer have a convex form; on the contrary, the torso of the goddess is slightly bent forward, as in Christian statuary. But there is no anxiety or torment here. This work is inspired by the very best of antiquity: voluptuousness governed by restraint, a cadenced love of life, modified by reason.

Now that Rodin has enlightened us on the meaning of the positioning of the body, let us return to our armchairs, in the company of François Roustang. See if you can retain a bit of that love of life and Greek voluptuousness in your posture. Once you've found a position that suits you, allow yourself to ask the question again: how do you imagine energy? Is energy, for you, something you stock up in a reservoir and then consume, like gasoline? Something you compress, then release, like steam? Something that's constantly circulating, like an electric current or a fluid; or, to return to François Roustang's image, "like a breath"? Is energy something you produce and that comes from you, or something that passes through you, or again, something that exists outside you, that you ride on? It may seem like a small thing, but it's crucial. The way you think of energy is decisive, because your way of imagining energy will either galvanize you or not; will either make it possible for you to refresh it easily or not. In a word, your imagination is at the heart of your life. It's what forms your body image and structures the nature of the exchanges between yourself and the world; it's what weaves you. The imagination nourishes the will, by supplying it with images. Imagining that energy is solid, liquid, or gas gives you access to different types of energy. If you think of energy as an individual tank, on the model of fossil fuels or a combustion engine, you will have a limited tank, and will have to find outside sources of energy to "fill up." If you think of it as an element, along the model of the sea, then rhythm will override quantity in your imagination. And gradually you will begin to take on the idea that energy can be renewed without effort, like the breaking and backwash of the waves, which never cease to move. If energy is a breath, you need only breathe in to get more energy, and breathe out as long as possible, to empty your lungs and allow your energy to renew itself, as one clears the air in a room by opening the windows. So examine your images of energy and test out François Roustang's proposition: rather than thinking of energy in terms of tension and explosion, experiment with the breath, which circulates freely. The gods of the wind, with no apparent effort, were always the most powerful. Aeolus has a more decisive effect on the life of Ulysses in the *Odyssey* than either Poseidon or Zeus. Energy like the breath, like the sea, like lightning: whichever image you choose, give it a chance and try to live it, naively, genuinely. Let each one inhabit you, try them out, as you might try out a new car, with no speed limit. Try to find out which one works best for you, energizes you most, makes your life easiest. Look for the image that's most comfortable for you. Comfort, in this method, is everything. The point of departure and the point of arrival: phobias are resolved indirectly, out of the corner of one's eye, without thinking about it. They will be resolved because they dissolve into something far greater than themselves, or they disappear. And hypnosis, explains François Roustang, is nothing other than "the practice of an art of action that would cure us of many purely fabricated ills. If, under its influence, problems are re-solved as though by magic, this is simply because the person needed to act them out, instead of torturing themselves by thinking about it." Obviously I can't hypnotize you here; this is a book, not a therapist's room. But the goal of hypnosis is to in-duce a state with nothing illusory or artificial about it, which allows one to resolve with disconcerting ease difficulties that one believed to be insurmountable. There is no reason why we can't reach this state by ourselves, more gradually than through hypnosis—or at least catch a glimpse of it and understand its principles. The first of these principles being: stop thinking.

6

The Art of Gliding

Water like a skin
That no one can harm
PAUL ÉLUARD

You'd know him anywhere—the distinctive hat, the long gray hair, the uncut nails to avoid touching anything with his over-sensitive fingers: all these details give him away, but no one recognizes him here, because here no one knows him. It's true, he's ventured a long way from his familiar universe. For one evening, the walls of books will make way for walls of water, the rows of university desks will yield to banks of sand, and the logic of meaning to the thrill of great waves. For once, the philosopher who is so fiercely protective of his privacy and so very much in love with silence will plunge into the crowd of overexcited young people at the Grand Rex cinema, who like him have come to "Nuit de la Glisse" (literally, "the Night of

Slipping," or sliding or gliding), a film festival devoted to surfing and extreme sports. Why has he "slipped" into this event, to which he is suited neither by age nor by temperament? Because he has written a book on Leibniz called *Le Pli* (The Fold) and surfing is exactly about that, about catching the fold, or groove, letting yourself slide into the wave. And isn't the purpose of philosophy to explicate, i.e., to explore the folds in the world? In Latin it's the same word (*ex-plicare*): to explicate is to unfold. Philosophy can learn from surfing, so Gilles Deleuze has accepted an invitation from the magazine *Surf Session* to come and discover the most spectacular films about this discipline. In *Pourparlers* (Negotiations), he unfolds his idea:

> Movements, in sport as in customs, change. For a long time we lived with an energy-based concept of movement: either there's a pressure point, or you are yourself the source of the movement. Running, throwing a weight, etc.: that's effort, resistance, with a point of origin, a lever. But today movement seems to be defined less and less in terms of the insertion of a leverage point. All the new sports—surfing, wind sailing, hang gliding...are based on insertion into a preexisting wave. The origin is no longer the point of departure, it's a way of putting oneself into orbit. How you gain access to the movement of a great wave, or an upward column of air, how you "join" instead of being yourself the source of effort—all this is fundamental.

"Joining," slotting in, slipping into the fold, means no longer having to start the movement, just continuing it. Slotting in is always a delicate art, but it's easier than having to start from scratch. It requires turning all one's attention outward, listening, first of all, to the world rather than to oneself, adapting to what is already there, and considering oneself a tiny part of the whole, which one can weave gracefully in and out of. You also need a sense of rhythm to enter into the dance rather than imposing your own tempo. All this without effort, since there is no pressure point, and no lever effect: the movement is already there, you don't need to create it—just find the right position and glide on the wave.

But there is also an elementary aspect: while you can have an airwave, or a wave of water, there is no such thing as an earth wave; no one surfs on an earthquake or a mud slick. And yet, among the "new sports" there is also skateboarding, basically surfing on concrete, which, though it doesn't use an actual wave, should nevertheless be considered a kind of gliding, of slipping into the urban landscape. The skater weaves everywhere, introducing a glide where one wouldn't normally exist: on staircases, ramps, benches, etc., transforming every obstacle into both a pushing-off point and an imaginary wave. The skater seems to have arisen from the ancient model of energy, and yet he behaves like a modern surfer. He brings the idea of the wave into the townscape, sets concrete in motion, lifts it with the powerful breath of imagination. Here we find a very particular case of what Gaston Bachelard calls dynamic imagination, as though the power of the oceanic metaphor, the dream of the wave could actually sweep across the concrete urban landscape and bring it to life, start an interior movement that might soften it sufficiently to turn it into a wave.

On snow it's a bit different, but not much: the mountain is experienced as an ocean, where the slope and the momentum it gives transform bumps into waves. Downhill skiing has always been seen as a "gliding" sport, unlike cross-country skiing, which is based on effort. Sailing too: a sailboat seeks the wind, adjusts to a current it doesn't create. Gliding, whether on water, on air, or on snow, always involves trying to ally oneself with a wave one has not created oneself. It's no less tiring than other sports. An hour of surfing is usually spent mostly paddling and falling. But it is more immediately exhilarating because one is in direct contact with the element. Water and air, at the moment when they're most dangerous, as wave or wind, carry us along. Then it's no longer a sport, in which individuals compete through the energy they create, but principally a sensory and imaginary experience, an elementary pleasure. The aesthetic is more important than performance, and the surfer's main priority is to "take" the wave well, to cut a beautiful line across it. As for people who surf the "big ones," who throw themselves into waves in excess of twenty meters, their pursuit of the giant wave is less like chasing after a record than the quest of a hunter or an explorer. "When the sea is calm, when there are no waves," confides Laird Hamilton, the legendary surfer, "I feel like a knight with no dragon to slay." Subduing sea monsters is, of course, sport, but most importantly it is a mythical dream.

Joining an existing movement, a preexisting wave, is not unique to gliding sports (or board sports, as they're more commonly known). In horse riding too, animal energy preexists the rider. In rodeo, you literally surf the animal wave. There are two ways of learning to ride a horse, the philosopher Henri Bergson used to say to his friends. The first is that of the sergeant major, who seeks to dominate, master, and break the animal, to subdue it: tension, effort, injury, wounds. The other way is to do the opposite, to mold oneself to the movement of the horse, to follow it with suppleness, to "sympathize" with it. To obey the animal so that one day you will be in a position to give it orders, and not the other way around. Horse riding is also a "gliding sport"—you surf on the movement of the horse—with the one crucial difference that you may eventually end up being able to steer the animal wave, but never that of the ocean.

Finally, the opposition proposed by Deleuze, between ancient sports founded on effort and new sports founded on gliding, is not so inflexible as you might think. As with horse riding, there are always two ways of looking at the world of action: the "sergeant major" version, with force, purely mechanically; and the "dancer" version. Think back to Zidane for a moment: his "grace" rests primarily on his way of passing in between, inserting himself into the movement of his opponents, avoiding them without touching them, as though surfing over them. He looks like he's dancing because he never enters into violent contact with his opponent; he attains his goal without brutality, softly, lightly, in rhythm. He explains, when discussing the art of heading the ball, that what gifted headers like Zamorano have is a sense of timing. They always jump at the right moment, and follow the trajectory of the ball. It's not a question of size, it's not enough just to be tall. You need to sense the right moment. Like a dancer. People who excel in the "old sports" practice them as though they were gliding sports rather than contact sports. Zidane is a surfer; he can catch the wave of the ball and think of the game as an element or a wave. You may think a soccer pitch is just a flat surface, with two dimensions. For a great player it's an ocean, a living surface, in three dimensions.

Time too is a wave. Tennis players know something about this, because for them matches have no predetermined length. Andre Agassi says there is a moment in a match when you physically feel two opposing currents, two forces, one drawing you toward victory, the other toward defeat. The player is at the delta of these two forces, their meeting point, and whether you turn one way or the other can sometimes hang on a single point. They are like currents in the ocean. You have to be able to seize them. And not force, hurry, or seek to accelerate time. Acting can also mean waiting, even when you are in the process of acting. You have to negotiate time as you would negotiate a bend in the road, follow its curve, or its descent, not try to resist it or to hurry it along. In tennis you ride time as you would ride a wave.

In the end it all comes down to attitude, imagination and...
prepositions. You can be "against," or "in" or "on" or "with." You
can strain, struggle, compete, or you can relax, accept, and give
in. It's like learning a foreign language. Here too you have two
ways of doing it: the first is the one used in school, the sergeant
major's method with grammar lessons, vocabulary lists, tests,
and grades. It doesn't usually get you very far: even after years
of effort it's still impossible to have a reasonable conversation
with a native speaker. As though you were to try to surf while
staying on the beach, or swim while staying at the edge of
the water. The second way is total immersion: spending a few
months in the country, understanding nothing at the start,
basking in the language from dawn till dusk, observing, soak-
ing yourself in it, imitating, muddling along, until one day you
end up speaking it. With ease. In English we speak of *fluency*: to
be *fluent* is to be fluid in a language, to allow it to flow through
you, without having to think about every word before saying it.
Language is a flux, a stream, a wave to be surfed; you have to
trust it. To learn to speak a language you have to *speak*, and act
as though you already knew it. The same goes for dance: you
learn not by watching but by doing. Not to say that you shouldn't
take dance classes, but you can only correct a movement once
you've started it. You can only correct a phrase if it has already
been said. Desire, not scholarly obligation, is what teaches us to
speak or to dance.

So "pretending" is also a condition of success. In order to

learn to speak a language, I have to start by pretending I know how to speak it. Bergson is saying the same thing when he recommends that we yield to the "grace of horse riding"; in other words, that we act as if we already knew how to do it by slipping supplely into the movement of the horse, without resisting. It means trusting the body, and allowing it to learn by itself, to enter into horse-becoming, to use Deleuze's expression, instead of clinging fearfully to one's human-being.

There is so much we can learn from animals, especially when inserting ourselves into an element. You need only look at the metaphors we use to evoke a sense of ease: to be as free as a bird, to feel like a fish in water. These are not just metaphors, they are examples to be followed. The bird is, above all, a wing, a sail in search of the wind. The fish flies in the water, its fins are both wings and oars; it can also hover, or accelerate suddenly, using both its strength and its ability to glide. It surfs in three dimensions. A dolphin does it both on the surface and underwater, almost in four dimensions. The equipment of gliding sports is inspired by animal forms and properties. Here, imitation is the rule. Lightness and resistance in the materials, the balance between flexibility and toughness in the flippers, the ribs in the fins, the improvement of the gliding movement through the tapered shape and waxing of the boards. But above all, the attitude of the practitioners of these "new sports" follows animal models.

Even freediving, which is based on the suppression of the respiratory reflex, can be thought of less as an unnatural effort made against nature in a hostile environment and more as a nat-ural insertion into a welcoming element. To the scientists who covered him in electrodes, riddled him with X-rays, and bom-barded him with analyses in an attempt to understand how, without breathing apparatus, he could descend to a depth of over one hundred meters, and withstand a pressure of more than ten atmospheres, Jacques Mayol explained with an amused smile: "When I dive, it's not complicated. I feel as though I'm in love with the water! But how do you say 'love' in mathematical language?" You can't say it, or rather you can't measure it. But you can feel it and see it. Because he didn't take humans for his model, Jacques Mayol thought of himself not as a sportsman but as a dolphin, or rather a *Homo delphinus*, a man in the process of dolphin-becoming, and even of dolphin re-becoming, since he thought of his deep underwater adventures as a return to our repressed aquatic origins. After all, our cells swim about in salt water, don't they? The living cell, since Charles Bernard, has been thought of as an interior micro-ocean. Our lack of fur, the shape of our noses, and even the tears that constantly bathe our eyes surely indicate clearly that we first appeared not on earth, but in water. How else can we explain our capacity to hold our breath underwater for long periods or all the things we have in common with marine mammals—in particular the "blood shift," which allows us to descend below fifty meters in water without our lungs collapsing under the pressure—in short: how can we explain Jacques Mayol? One thing is certain: he himself experiences freediving as an insertion into the sea, rather than a struggle against it; as a loving relationship, not a conflictual one. Exactly like people who choose to learn horse riding by following the movement of the horse, he learned to free dive by taking as his master—or mistress, almost—a female dolphin called Clown, whom he met at the Seaquarium in Miami, Florida. He says he felt himself genuinely fall head over heels in love with her, "as though Clown were a woman! In particular, I had that very special feeling all lovers get, that I'd known her for a very long time. And I swear it was the same for her!" He attributes his ease in the water, his relaxed way of being, his elegance and the efficiency of his movements to her, but above all, to his love of the element, his love of the water, and deep down, right deep down, to love, period. "There's a calm deep inside you. And at the bottom of that calm—there's love. The dolphins taught me that. It's thanks to them I broke all my records."

His main adversaries—and partners—in this conquest of the deep, the Italian Enzo Maiorca and the American Robert Croft, who each broke the world record on several occasions, give you the feeling they opted for the first way, training based on conscious methodical effort, and the invention of techniques that made it possible either to increase their lung capacity or to inhibit their breathing reflex. Croft practiced lung packing, or air packing, which, once you have filled your lungs right up, consists of continuing to pump air by puffing out the cheeks and sending it down to the lungs. Maiorca, on the other hand, used hyperventilation, which consists of speeding up the rate of inhalation, so as to greatly reduce the level of carbon dioxide in the blood, thereby delaying the respiratory reflex, which is governed by this level. He also trained by very slowly climbing and descending a three-story flight of stairs without breathing, wearing huge lead belts. "It's even harder than under water, because under water you really have no choice but to hold out, whereas there you could simply open your mouth and breathe. The temptation is terrible. You have to resist. That's how you train your willpower."

I'm not for a moment trying to reduce Croft and Maiorca to representatives of a caricatural, strength-based approach, while handing Mayol a monopoly on subtlety and gentleness. But training on the ground, suffering in stairways, thinking at every step about not breathing—it just doesn't have the same attraction as playing for hours in a huge tank with someone you love. It's the negative world of will against the positive world of desire: on the one hand you resist the temptation to breathe, on the other you pursue the pleasure of the game. "You have to resist" doesn't have the same ring to it as "deep down there is calm, and love." This love without an object is a state of well-being rather than a feeling. It's closer to meditative bliss than to intense passion. It's a form of profound peace with oneself and with the world, conducive to relaxation, to forgetfulness of self and thought. An impersonal and timeless experience, which puts the necessity to breathe on the back burner. Jacques Mayol:

> The first big mistake to avoid is struggling against the passing seconds. As soon as there's struggle, there's conflict, and

therefore contraction, both physical and psychic. Which brings about the opposite of what you want, which is to go with the flow, allowing yourself to be carried along, in a state of total relaxation. To hold your breath properly, paradoxical though it may sound, you have to not think about holding it. You have to do it without thinking. You have to become the act itself. Like an animal.

Jacques Mayol doesn't resist the water; he passes between the droplets, lets himself be carried along in the flow. He doesn't resist the desire to breathe; he forgets to think about it. It's not even enough to stop thinking about it—he actually imagines himself to be a dolphin. His thought is neutralized, but his imagination is active. He doesn't float in the ether of unconsciousness, he swims in the bliss of his dreams. Like a dolphin in the water.

7

Stop Thinking

Life can be explored but not explained

FRANÇOIS ROUSTANG

October 19, 1983. 2:24 p.m. The October sun casts its golden glow over the Isle of Elba. It could still be summer. On board the *Corsaro* there's total silence. The sea is beautiful, we're a mile out from Pareti. In exactly six minutes Jacques Mayol will shed the 110-pound cast-iron weight whose job is to take him down into the deep. The countdown begins. Seated on the deck of the boat, with his legs in the water, he watches the departure of the safety divers, who will position themselves at various depths to watch out for him and help, if needed. What's he thinking about? Maybe his friend Yoshizumi Azaka, whom he met in 1970 in a temple in Japan, at Izu, and who taught him Zen by repeating *"No thinking! No thinking!"* while striking him on the shoulder with a stick—the famous Zen master's stick, for banishing stray ideas and bringing the attention of the meditator to the here and now. Or perhaps he's thinking of his friend Clown. In playing with her, he realized that when he had negative thoughts, she felt it and distanced herself from him, as though to say that he needed to get rid of them, to clean his spirit. The dolphin and the monk were in agreement: "No thinking!," as though thinking were something that could be done on its own, a purely mechanical activity, a compulsion or a tic one could get rid of at leisure, by a simple gesture, like turning a doorknob. No thinking. Easy to say. Maybe Mayol recalls Dr. Cabarrou, the French doctor who warned that below fifty meters, the thoracic cage of a freediver holding their breath must necessarily suffer fatal collapse. And yet he has done it. He's been down below fifty meters. Enzo Maiorca has even been below sixty meters. Mayol thinks again about his first attempt to break Maiorca's record. It was at Freeport, in the Bahamas. As he dived with his eyes shut, he had asked one of his safety divers to give him a tap on the back at fifty meters, so he knew how far he'd gone. But this contact had also brought him out of his trance. He had opened his eyes, seen the flag attached to the cable, ten meters below him, marking the depth Maiorca had reached, and stopped. There was nothing he could do to compensate: his ears just wouldn't go down any farther. This abrupt reminder of reality, the sudden intervention of thought, had broken his momentum. He had to come back up. It was only a postponement, and he did finally go down farther than sixty meters, but he never forgot the incident. The greatest danger for a freediver at this depth is thinking. Maiorca's best was sixty-two meters. Robert Croft went down below sixty-four meters, then sixty-six meters. At this point Mayol decided to spend several months in the temple at Izu, to prepare himself for the record in a way quite unlike the insistence on honing the physique, or by forcing the breath. Instead, he would learn not to think. Non-thinking, combined with yogic breathing exercises, would give him the last word when, on September 11, 1970, he went down to seventy-six meters. And it was the last word because in December 1970 the Confédération Mondiale des Activités Subaquatiques (CMAS), the diving federation that had until then overseen attempts at record breaking, decided to abolish the discipline for safety reasons. Good-bye sport, hello experimentation.

Back in October 1983, could Mayol be thinking of Dr. Roger Lescure, who deemed it criminal to pursue this kind of experience, because at eighty meters, in his estimation, the freediver had only a few seconds of conscious life left? What is Mayol thinking about, with only a few seconds of the countdown to go? Impossible to say. 2:30. He lifts his hand. He positions his nose peg, grasps the iron bar hanging in front of him, takes a normal breath, no forcing, and vanishes into the deep. He's fifty-six years old. The cutoff disk awaits him at 105 meters. If he's properly prepared, he won't be thinking about it.

Not thinking about a challenge isn't always enough. Before she goes out on stage, Hélène Grimaud gets stage fright, which she prefers to call the "adrenalin phenomenon." Her heart races, blood drains from her extremities. Her breath shortens. And yet she's thinking of nothing. She is both concentrated and vacant. Her stomach pounds. Her legs scarcely hold her up. As a child she played with pleasure, fearlessly. What happened? It all started just before she recorded her first album. A mad choice, a piece that was too difficult for her, in the opinion of all her teachers. A whim. A dream. A few minutes before entering the studio, her body let her down, the "adrenalin phenomenon" took hold of her for the first time, and has never let her go. Ever since then, her body thinks for her, and like a scratched record, it goes over and over the same groove of fear, which is definitively scored into her, burned into her, forever. How can she stop her body thinking? Willpower won't work, and neither will thinking. She uses her breath, and thinks simply about completely emptying her lungs, and drawing in large belly breaths. Her blood rushes back, she re-centers herself. She replaces thinking with imagination and lines up some mental projections. She fixes her attention on three things, always the same ones. She concentrates on the first, then the second, then all three together, like the three cherries in a slot machine. She explains:

> This technique draws me into the rhythm, till I reach illumination. The principle is to perfectly control one's breath while focusing one's attention on the passing images. When you reach the alpha brain state, you enter a trance, the ideal rhythm, like with Buddhist mantras. The aim, as you con-

tinue the exercise, is for the brain to stop formulating distinct thoughts. There's another exercise I really like: imagine
yourself in a place you love, or that you'd love to visit, the
top of a tower, for example, from which you have a lovely
view out on the world. You see a staircase: at the bottom of
the staircase you see a room; at the end of the room is a
door; you open the door; you go into the room and there
you find something or someone. What you find, usually, is a
loved one, or someone who's died; in fact, your own inner
voice.

In other words, she practices self-hypnosis. Therapist François
Roustang confirms the benefits of this method. Focusing on
one's breath is the best means of coming back into the body, of
suppressing troublesome thoughts. Unease always comes from
rigidity blocking the flow of life. Breathing well, breathing
slowly and deeply, is a way of reestablishing this flow. To suspend his thought entirely, Roustang uses three exercises: the
first consists of fixing his gaze on a limited part of an object—for
example, the point of a pencil, the handle of a cup, or the pattern
on a cushion. The aim is to isolate what you're looking at from
its context, banishing everything else into the background haze.
In the second exercise you transport yourself in your imagination to somewhere you love, in the country, or in the town, or
the mountains, it doesn't matter where, as long as it's a place
you associate with pleasant feelings. In the third you use language in a nonsensical way. This is the most unsettling exercise.

"This is a strange experience because it's expressed in absurdities: 'Take a path you don't know, to reach an unknown place, to do something you're incapable of doing.' Phrases like this, though apparently meaningless and highly risky, once heard and put into practice open up a space of freedom and pleasure, where existence can be renewed." Using language in this way means you can't visualize anything precise, and this is exactly the point of the exercise: to reestablish a sense of the possible. Not by having a very clear goal or image, but by accepting confusion and vagueness. And this is perhaps the most surprising and fertile idea in this method: anyone who hopes to find a way to act and to reinvent themselves should not start by fixing clear goals, but rather should start in a floating, indeterminate state, in a fog, which will allow action to take shape. Night makes the light shine, just as the cloud creates the bolt of lightning.

It's not just about overcoming stage fright. You can actually learn to stop thinking any time you have to act. Excessive thinking can contaminate a whole existence and even threaten it. Hélène Grimaud explains how her meeting with a great violinist, Gidon Kremer, at the Lockenhaus Chamber Music Festival, completely changed her life and her relationship with the piano. Having previously prided herself on her intuition, and allowed herself to be guided by the ideas that simply arose from it, after this encounter she began to analyze her own playing. And as she began to consider all the possibilities, she gradually cut herself off from reality:

I asked myself so many questions that I stopped being able to detach myself from the score, or step back enough to actually get on with playing. Some days, I felt like I understood, I would briefly sense what could be and would be, I knew exactly what it was meant to be. But between those brief moments of lucidity, those rare illuminations, I was going around with my eyes closed. I thrashed about trying to solve my difficulties, sometimes for weeks, without finding a solution.

She began to suffer from genuine instrumental paralysis, and eventually fell ill.

I couldn't work, except on the score. I spent my time reading, always reading; books, and especially music. I was entirely focused on my inertia, and I wouldn't leave the apartment. I marinated, ruminated, despaired, I was weighed down by a great jumble of fictional characters, of different acquaintances. I didn't want to see anyone. I was tormented by a sense of powerlessness, or worse still, of uselessness. My suffering was like an action in itself and the contemplation of this suffering was an abyss. A great black hole took shape in my chest. The hole didn't communicate with infinite space, or the cosmos, or the dizzying architecture of music but, like a hole in the bottom of a boat, with the murky waters of the deep, and it drank up that darkness too. I was living through an experience akin to self-dispossession. The abandon of the self by oneself, after the departure of everyone else. In 1989, at the Festival de La Roque-d'Anthéron, where I was due to appear for the third time, I was in a total slump. I believed, I really believed at that time, that I would never get out of it. For the first time in my life I felt a wild, brutal, irrepressible desire to disappear.

Rumination, which stands in the way of action, an excess of interpretation that stops one from experiencing, a loss of curiosity for what's going on in the world, an end to the lightness of being: Hélène Grimaud neatly diagnoses this major crisis in her existence. By overanalyzing her playing, she stepped out of life, off the pitch. When they ask how you are, the Swiss aptly say: "How's it playing?" Once you've stopped playing, everything stops.

Hélène Grimaud, through sheer intelligence, lost her instinct. How do you get out of such an impasse? How do you rediscover your ability to play? François Roustang warns that you're obviously not going to cure someone of excessive analysis by excessively analyzing them. More thinking won't cure someone of too much thinking. First you must try to put an end to rumination,

which dwells on remorse, regrets and resentment. Then you must close down the route that leads us to search for the causes of and reasons for our problems. To do that, to stop thinking, or to succeed in no longer thinking, you need to have thought for a long time, tiring out your thought as you might tire out a wild horse in order to mount it.

Wear out your thinking, so you know from the inside that it's useless to you, so that at last you are ready to act.

*

Beware the trap of "I want to understand." In a chapter entitled "L'illusion du sens" (The Illusion of Meaning), Roustang writes: "The symptom is already isolating, it holds back life's flow, arrests us, and sets us apart. By focusing on it we run the risk of reinforcing it." The solution is not to dig into the problem until you're so deep you're stuck, or to keep going round and round it till you end up just turning in circles; it is to leave the problem where it is, there in the middle of everything else, one detail in a moving ensemble, rather than an immovable focal point, fixed, petrified by the desire to understand it.

In hypnosis therapy, everything is already there, and we allow what is indistinct to emerge, the wave of the whole range of thoughts, representations, feelings, perceptions, sensations: everything that produces a state of confusion into which we launch ourselves, without a compass or a rudder. The symptom is then submerged, carried off, loosed from its moorings and thus constrained to accept or to submit to all aspects of the shape or flow of life.

The "trance" of hypnosis is a "trans," a crossing, an intermediate state. The point of action is also a point of passage.

Which means that contrary to the entire psychoanalytical tradition, in order to feel better, you don't need to look at yourself, to waste time self-examining: "self-analysis is pernicious; you end up looking at yourself instead of living." The philosopher Ludwig Wittgenstein wrote in his *Secret Notebooks*, written during the First World War: "When you feel yourself coming up against a problem you need to stop thinking about it, otherwise you can't get free of it. You have to start thinking at the point where you can sit comfortably. Above all, do not insist! Difficult problems must resolve themselves before our eyes." But how can you resolve a problem without thinking about it? This idea is even stranger coming from a philosopher as focused on science and logic as Wittgenstein was. It is hard to see how a theorem, for example, could demonstrate itself. Would you not rather need to pay attention to it, in the strongest sense of the word? And if attention is something that can be paid, doesn't that suppose an effort? Teachers order you to "pay attention!," in the certainty that if only you'd make the effort you'd understand. Wittgenstein recommends the opposite: don't insist, don't get bogged down, stop thinking, let problems resolve themselves. "Before our eyes," he says. Just because we are not trying too hard doesn't mean we mustn't keep our eyes open. In keeping them open we pay a kind of attention that doesn't try to force anything, but is simply a "gaze," without tension. The secret of this "gaze" is comfort: "start thinking at the point where you feel you are sitting comfortably." Comfort first, then thought as a consequence of comfort. Comfort as a prerequisite to the resolution of any difficulty. If you want to feel at ease in your life, you need to start by getting comfortable in your chair. And then, a bit like at the cinema, as long as you don't try to intervene, you'll find your problems resolving themselves. This is a long way from the educational model of forced attention, authoritarian command, discipline above all else. It is only by renouncing the idea of solving the problem directly that we have a chance of getting rid of it. Wittgenstein says: "The solution to any problem you have in life is a way of life that makes the problem disappear." Roustang adds: "The solution to a human problem will never be found in a response to the question why."

*

When, after crossing between the towers of the World Trade Center eight times, during a display that lasted forty-five minutes, Philippe Petit finally came down from the wire, and was immediately arrested. The first question he was asked, by an American journalist, as he was being taken to the police station, was "Why?" To which Philippe Petit responded, without thinking: "There is no why." If there was a why, there would be no tightrope walkers. The tightrope walker is the response to a question that need not be asked. Who could find a reason to go and risk his life on a wire stretched 400 meters above ground? Reflection is the enemy of the tightrope walker: "Every thought on the wire leads to a fall." So, don't think. It's easy to say, but how can you think about not thinking? Instead of thinking about the void, you have to *do* it. Stop looking down; look straight out ahead. "The feeling of a second of immobility—if the wire grants it to you—is an intimate happiness. If no thought came to disturb this miracle, it would go on and on forever." But "the wind of our thoughts [is] more violent than the wind of balance." Thinking is the enemy. It need not even have any particular content. It is at the same time an imbalance, a wind, forever reborn and always on the attack. Thinking is moving out of the moment to look at yourself acting, leaving the point of action and projecting yourself into the past or the future—and projecting yourself when you are on a rope means falling. If you suspend a philosopher in a cage between the towers of Notre-Dame in Paris, says Montaigne, even if he sees that it is impossible to fall out, the sight of the extreme drop is bound to frighten and paralyze him. Or "if, between these two towers, one places a beam broad enough to walk along, there is no philosophical wisdom, however strong, that can give us the courage to walk it as we would do if it was on the ground. There are some people who can't even bear the thought of it." Pascal repeats Montaigne without quoting him, and recognizes the same domination of the imagination over reason. "If you stand the greatest philosopher in the world on a plank, however wide, if there is a precipice below him, though his reason will convince him that he is safe, his imagination will prove stronger. Many people cannot think of it without growing pale and sweating."

How does Philippe Petit manage not to give in to fear and the thought of fear, which is already vertigo? It's simple: he doesn't fight it. He tries neither to pick up this thought nor to move forward with it. He allows it to float, like everything else. Because reflection means tying oneself up. Re-flection is always a doubling up; the prefix "re" suggests an insistence, a consciousness that is stuck in a rut, folding the problem in upon itself: perforce... to force. When you pull on a knot every which way to undo it, you succeed only in making it tighter. Insistence makes the problem worse, or even creates the problem in the first place. Before acting, you have to unknot yourself. Don't think about it; don't do anything.

But how do you do nothing? And how can you think about not thinking, without thinking? It's a vicious circle. If I say to you: "Don't think about a frog," what else are you going to do? Fortunately, this contradiction disappears when you put it into practice. The secret of non-thinking is to appeal not to thought but to the body. No reasoning, just an action: simply finding the right position in the chair. Roustang again:

> Doing nothing means doing nothing in particular, not stopping on any particular thought or feeling or sensation. This doing nothing becomes letting things happen. Now, letting things happen is the equivalent of a state of receptivity without limitation. When you are open to everything and nothing, you really have no preferences, no wishes, and no plans whatsoever, what you touch and what you receive is pure

force of action. You are at the source of the action. The individual who just lets things happen is constantly adjusting themselves to what comes toward them, and that's the beginning—and already the fullness—of action.

The hardest thing to accept with this concept of action is that it isn't the outcome of thinking, or the result of a project or decision, and that it seems to make us spectators rather than actors in our own lives. But if we think back to Françoise Sagan's "blessed moments," to Yannick Noah's "rare moments," or to Hélène Grimaud's "visitation," it is clear that when "it works," when "it takes," when you reach your point of action, "it" works of its own accord, "it" takes us, "it" happens to us as if it were nothing to do with us. The idea is thus to rediscover the physical state of indifferent attention in order to notice what is taking form, to be present at the appearance, not simply of a project (which would again be a thought turned toward the future), but of an action (the first step, in the present, of the execution of this "plan" that isn't a "plan" because it is already under way). This might seem to contradict the call of action, when you're not always free to just take your time, when a crisis demands speed. But this state, once you're familiar with it and can identify it, can be rediscovered instantaneously, as Zidane shows when he talks about his Panenka in the 2006 World Cup Final. The decision coincides with the execution. He knew what he had to do even as he did it. It was the right decision, because it was not so much considered as received. Zidane, like Socrates, obeyed his inner voice, his "genius." Once you have found the right wavelength, all you have to do is connect to it. It is like a radio station—you just have to find the right frequency.

*

The primary model for "facility" is animal. Instinct succeeds without thinking, unlike intelligence, which is often clumsy because of its conscious and indirect nature. When you have to think in order to act you lose the advantage of immediacy. Instinct asks no questions; it is what it does, no more, no less. Intelligence thinks the action, dominates it, and thus is always at risk of preventing it. Instinct is a form of idiocy, of blissful ignorance, which succeeds without thinking. What is really difficult, for an intelligent being, is reaching this state of idiocy without losing any of one's intelligence, constructing a second nature in which intelligence becomes intuition. This natural state is what athletes aim for, and actors as well: "When I played Danton," Gérard Depardieu says, "I was guillotined on the first day of filming. My head was gone, I couldn't think, I had nothing to do but be." It was very clever of the director, Andrzej Wajda, because that way he was allowing his actor to act not with his brain but with his gut. Depardieu appreciated this move, and even made it a life principle that he could apply to the rest of existence:

No more ideas about anything. It's a win-win. When you feel a certain *joie de vivre*, for example, if you start thinking you're happy, or worse, asking yourself why you're happy or why you're not unhappy, you are already less able to enjoy the *joie de vivre*. You lose an essential part of it. *Joie de vivre* simply has to be experienced in the present moment.

This immediate experience, without introspection, may sound a bit brutal, even animal, but that doesn't bother Depardieu. "I never try to appear kind or sympathetic. I simply live. And I never calculate." No effort, ever, just the ebb and flow of life, without a backward glance. Ceasing to think allows one to commit to the present. For an actor, the difficulty lies in reaching this state of calm indifference in spite of the presence of other people, whether that's the technical crew in filmmaking or the audience in theater. Depardieu says:

> It's always terrifying to be alone on stage in front of the audience, not speaking. Forcing yourself simply to *be*. That's why actors in the theater often rush in too quickly, too loud. Régy taught me to take my time, to play with the wait, feel the silence, till the moment when the words simply have to come out. In the end it's less about saying something than knowing how to hold back.

Ceasing to think is a remedy for, as well as a test of, impatience. By not projecting himself into the future, the actor acquires density, truth, presence, a form of splendid slowness, the tranquility of a wild animal, and therein lies the richness of his style. Even if theater director Claude Régy was one of the people who set him on this path, Depardieu considers it a training that has very little to do with teaching: "You don't learn anything at school, you learn things with your body. Through watching, through breathing, through feeling." It's more a question of attention and perception than of knowledge or work. Depardieu is making a case here for a form of ignorance:

> I'm much more at ease when I don't know much about things. I don't explain them, they come of their own accord, without barriers, with no agenda. Everything comes to me loose. It's like when you throw grapes into a vat. One fine day it starts to bubble. Or not. It takes or it doesn't. There are good years and bad years. You can use a whole load of artificial stuff for making wine. I make wine the classic way. Let's just say I put my trust in nature. Nature is always right if you don't contradict her. It comes out the way it comes out.

It might surprise people that an actor who is accustomed to performing the great works, in a variety of languages, should be so unconcerned with the question of meaning. Doesn't performance necessarily require having an idea about the text? Don't you have to have reached the meaning hidden in a work through profound analysis before proposing, as they say, your own reading? Depardieu explains why exactly the opposite is true:

When I act in a foreign language, I don't care if I don't understand the text of my character. The punctuation is more important to me than the words. I perform more like a musician than an actor. When I read the part of Cyrano, I feel the music long before the words. In *I Want to Go Home*, by Alain Resnais, we were filming in English, and I didn't understand a word of what I was saying, I just acted out the situation, in the present moment. It all went really well till the day Resnais translated some sentences of the dialogue and explained the meaning of my words to me. That was it, I couldn't act after that, I couldn't be true, I was paralyzed by what I had to say. We had to film the scene dozens of times.

Not understanding what he's saying is not only *not* an obstacle for Gérard Depardieu, it's actually an opportunity. In order to perform, he needs not to focus on what he has to say or do. After all, no one expects a violin to understand the music it makes possible. The actor is like an instrument through which the music passes. He may feel it is beautiful, as long as he doesn't know how or why. Paradoxically, it is this distance from the content of the text that allows one to give the truest interpretation, to resonate with it:

When I read Saint Augustine, even more than the text, which is often quite demanding, the audience needed to feel its vibrations, to touch them deep within their soul. Beyond the words, they were in a state of prayer with themselves.

For me it was like reading a story to a child who's falling asleep, led by our voice into its own world, where the imagination can do its work.

What is true for a text or for the scene is also true in life, and most especially in love: "The minute you try to control it, it's dead, it ages suddenly and the flame dies." Depardieu is not on the side of the will, or of effort; he is on the side of desire and what is natural. Through his words and his actions, Gérard Depardieu, actor/thinker, but above all thinker in action, advocates a kind of generalized negligence that makes him look primal in the eyes of imbeciles, but which is the sign of a higher intuition that says no to analytical reason and yes to the genius of life. "Of course you can give analysis a go, I did it for thirty years before I realized that in the end it was just one more self-indulgence. If you dwell on your regrets, your remorse, your grievances, you end up saturated, and you can't open your arms to life." It's almost like listening to François Roustang, with whom this profession of faith would chime perfectly, since he himself affirms:

It is one of the characteristics of life that it can never be understood; you can never completely grasp its complexity. The only true thought is the one that is prepared to plunge into life, with no turning back. Thus what might look like idiocy in fact becomes intelligence in action. The thought is accomplished once it falls mute in the silence of action.

And this is why François Roustang prefers hypnosis to straightforward analysis. Hypnosis allows one to get back to oneself, or rather to put one's self back into the world, in its place and in perspective. Hypnosis offers the experience of self-forgetfulness. We forget the self that is beset with problems, and in so doing, we rid it of that which is weighing on it, and bring it back to its fundamental substance: being alive. To be alive is to be no one, to be life, and nothing but. Not life in general, but my life, that life that flows through me, which is myself. "Myself" then becomes just a detail in a far greater ensemble. The Greeks called it a cosmos, a world in which each being is in its place, and happy to be there. "When someone is able to reduce themselves to the state of just being alive, then they are already cured. Because they re-situate themselves in their own body, in relation to their own body, re-situate themselves in relationship to their milieu, to the environment as a whole... That's enough." No need to aim for any goal, not even that of being cured. If I had a problem, it's now resolved. If I *was* a problem, it melted away, as I did, in something much larger: life. "You don't know what is happening, but if you stay calm, many things do happen."

You reach your goal by forgetting it. Or, rather, once we renounce a goal, it comes toward us. "The arrow, before it even leaves the bow, is already at the center of the target [...] there isn't really any distance between the one and the other, otherwise it would be impossible to shoot and reach the goal with your eyes closed." This presupposes the "abandon of all intentionality, the loss of the self that takes aim and directs the operation, in short, an impersonality that participates in the movement and is the finished gesture, and cannot be distinguished from it." You have to know how to wait. This waiting has nothing to do with fear, indecision, or, as for Hélène Grimaud, perfectionism. It's a way of respecting the idea that the time for action is born out of the action itself rather than out of us. To put it differently, if I put myself in the position of desiring nothing, if I bracket off my fear and my impatience, then the rhythm of things will be dictated by the length of time natural to them. It's a rather vegetal approach, but the affairs of mankind also have their seasons and duration, which should be respected. If an action isn't ripe, if it's not yet time, there's no point in forcing the decision. It's not I who take the decision and force my will on the world, but it is I who, by stepping aside, put myself at the world's disposal and decide to listen to its demands. Action will arise from total renunciation.

Most human problems that cannot be resolved by reflection can easily be resolved through action. Take shoelaces, for instance; it is much easier to show children how to tie their laces than to explain to them with words. Here, explaining involves doing. In the same way, if you want to understand how to tie shoelaces, the best thing is to just give it a go. Then undo them. And do them again. Certain difficulties can be resolved only by getting your hands dirty. It's your hands that learn to tie your laces. If thought plays any part, it's inside the action, thanks to it. What the hands understand is how to do without the head, to use it sparingly. A skill that is directly inscribed in your body is more easily acquired and preserved. We often take the example of the bicycle: balance can't be thought about; you find it by falling, and then by not falling, and finally you get it and never forget. The body's knowledge is what remains after you've forgotten everything. And to be more exact: it's what is left *because you've forgotten*. There is a way of forgetting that preserves, and which is called habit. You don't have to think about it to summon it. That knowledge is always there, close at hand and even in your hand, in your body, available, easy: whether it's cycling, driving, or reading a foreign language. When you've learned your lesson well you never forget it. And contrary to what you might think, "doing nothing" is an apprenticeship of this kind.

Artists are familiar with this phenomenon. When Picasso writes: "I do not seek, I find," this is not the statement of an arrogant genius, but rather the avowal of a determined and modest worker, who recognizes the impossibility of making the slightest connection between effort spent looking and the event of discovery. It is not enough just to seek in order to find—this is the tough law of the artist's task. You can miss your target a thousand times, and never hit the bull's-eye, and not even get close to it. Roustang writes:

> Brahms used to shut himself up for days on end and wait, before starting to write, till he found himself in a state he himself called hypnotic. In this state, he knew not to seek, just to let himself find. If such creators do find, it is because they've stopped looking or because their seeking has reached

a point at which it is clear that it is pointless. All their trying and their effort have led to a moment of despair that they will never find anything. During a certain period of his life, Picasso would get up each morning quite certain that he had painted his last ever painting the previous day. Convinced he would never paint again, he could allow himself, in the evening, to be possessed by a frenzy of painting.

To find, you have to have abandoned all hope, have sincerely renounced both yourself and any aim. Then, "if you stay calm, many things do happen." And everything happens easily.

What is true for art is also true for life in general, during which each of us is in a permanent state of creation. If we wish to achieve real change, there's no point in relying on the will, or planning. The shortest route to understanding oneself does not pass via the self: "The solution to our problems lies outside, in a new way of apprehending our situation. For this, we need to allow everything around us to come find us." Roustang takes the example of a young woman who came to see him because she couldn't leave her own child in peace, and was constantly nagging him. "I invited her to cross her index fingers and wait for them to come apart, without any intention on her part, and without any desire to achieve this end. She let herself go to the point of forgetting entirely why she had even come. After a quarter of an hour or twenty minutes, her fingers separated and she wept." When she came back the next week she reported that her relationships had changed for the better, not just with her child, but with everyone around her. In other words, there's no point in thinking about it: a movement is enough. This is what Roustang wittily calls "the mystique of the café waiter," which consists of shouting "Coming through!" and of thrusting forward, without thinking about looking at the drinks he's carrying on his tray. "It's vital not to think, but to allow life in all its variety to show us the way."

*

Allowing life to take the orders, trusting in disorder and not being frightened of chaos, is perhaps the best definition of "French flair," a term born on the rugby pitch. In a couple of memorable matches, just when everything seemed lost, the French team suddenly, as though hit by their own personal thunderbolt, turned into a band of irresistible flickering lights, and set the pitch on fire. Take, for example, that stroke of collective genius that's gone down in the history of modern rugby as the "try from the end of the world." And indeed, on July 3, 1994, the French were a long way from home. In Auckland, New Zealand, to be precise, where they were playing the All Blacks, who were leading 20-16 three minutes from the end of the game. They had nothing to lose.

Behind the twenty-two-meter line, Philippe Saint-André, winger and captain of Les Bleus, picks up the ball and instead of doing the usual thing of kicking it into touch, abandons all logic and decides to take a direct run at the opponent. Surprising everyone, he takes out three players, is caught by the fourth, who's slow to bring him down; he stays on his feet waiting for support from the heavy brigade—the two props, Bénézech and Califano—then frees the ball for Gonzalez, who also decides to do something unexpected. Instead of joining the fray, as a good hooker should, he slips into the role of scrum-half and brings the ball to life, it comes to Deylaud, then to Benazzi. Benazzi too does something unusual for him; he opts for a feint by extending his arms, dodging a tackle, and neutralizing two opponents: "I think that was the first time I'd ever done anything like that, but we were in the heat of the moment and I just felt it could work." Ntamack, then Cabannes. Then it gets even crazier: Cabannes senses that Delaigue is behind him and judges his pass to the millimeter. It's beautiful, clean, fluid, the French seem to be a beat ahead in everything, they're inspired, bold, everything is turning out right for them. Delaigue cuts left, and looks for a split second as though he's used the ref to screen himself from an imminent tackle, then sidesteps and opens the way for Accoceberry. The line is still fifteen meters away, but Delaigue has his arms in the air. He knows his pass is perfect, that the moment has to work, and that in spite of the three All Blacks bearing down on him, the try must be made. Accoceberry just has to clutch the ball to his chest and dive. The line is there. But it's not over yet. He is not alone. On his left are Sadourny, along with Saint-André, who has kept up with the ball and is following the action somehow, despite being tackled right at the start of this passage of play. Laurent Cabannes describes what happened: "We'd lost all sense of the crowd, there was no noise, we were one meter from paradise, behind that ridiculous little line of chalk, and at that point there could be an off-side call, a scrum, anything." Accoceberry only has to score to go down in history, but he plays collectively and shifts the ball to Sadourny, who finishes the move. Eighty meters run, twenty-seven seconds played, ten French players have touched the ball. If anyone asks what French flair is, it's *that*. The French won with a move of utter brilliance at the very last moment. Champagne!

What's the formula for this kind of alchemy? Even the players themselves don't know. Accoceberry acknowledges: "You can't take the action apart when you are on the pitch, because everything happens very fast and you're only involved in it for a few seconds. Afterward, without television everything would be a bit of a blur. When you watch it again, it's incredible, because the whole move is perfect, like something you try in training and you know you can never reproduce." And yet Philippe Saint-André, who set up the try, thinks it's the fruit of a certain culture:

> It was the end of the match, we were at the other end of the world, the goal line was still a long way off. But for me, it was really a typically French try, a mixture of three-quarter advances, crossing passes, keeping close, *chisteras* [neat back passes], flair... That try represented the whole tradition and culture of French rugby, so that we're playing against an

Anglo-Saxon team, but at the eightieth minute we can score a try that comes from nowhere. It's an amazing memory!

And even if it is impossible to reproduce the try exactly, marked as it is with the seal of collective improvisation, you can pick out the principles that made it possible, the spirit and the panache of this game played "French style."

In fact, it wasn't the first time France had won the day through an exploit defying all logic *in extremis*. There must be an explanation for this phenomenon. Could the French have a monopoly on the collective stroke of genius? Serge Blanco, himself an icon of the French style of game, and generator of a try of the same type at the end of a legendary World Cup semifinal against Australia in 1987, pours cold water on such extravagant notions:

> What is "French flair" exactly? It's when you think all is lost and you say to yourself: we've nothing left to lose. It's even a kind of cowardice, this "French flair"...It means we create situations in which, because we believe all is lost, we manage to turn the situation around. So if we were truly honest with ourselves, why not play in the first minute the way we are capable of playing in the seventy-fifth minute?

Indeed. If French flair can be born out of a sense of powerlessness, if it's just another name for the energy of despair, then it's nothing much to be proud of. But French flair isn't just that. To put it simply, where the Anglo-Saxons play with reason, the French take a bet on their intuition. Pierre Villepreux, who was a player and then trainer for the French team, is considered one of the principal upholders of this tradition and says: "There was a time when, compared to the more pragmatic, stereotypical English game, France developed a more inventive style of play. 'French flair' was this way of taking the initiative, often in a surprising way. It required some intelligence in reading the situation, which not everyone is capable of." It is not therefore simply the fruit of chance or despair, but the ability of the whole team to act both as a unit and as a fluid ensemble of individuals, each of whom has the freedom to read the game and to adapt in real time to disorder. Whether "inspiration" or situational intelligence, call this capacity for improvisation what you will, the aim is to act on the pitch like a jazz ensemble, always poised to follow and support your partner for as long as is required. René Deleplace, who is considered the theoretician of "total rugby," the idea that led to French flair, was not just a rugby man (a player and then trainer in the fifties and sixties), he was also a teacher of mathematics and above all a musician (French horn). He was a proponent of the idea of perpetual motion rugby, of seeking harmony between the lines in an ongoing improvisation. He was basically the designer of French flair. The paradox of rugby is that even when it is being played intuitively, it requires constant awareness and a detailed knowledge of the rules. Even if improvisation is the capacity to bring order to disorder, it is not an uncertain science itself; it consists of a series of micro-decisions taken rapidly, but always with an eye to the evolution of the game in real time. In rugby, you never stop reflecting; you simply think and decide at the speed of the ball itself.

*

But in the end the real inventor of French flair was Descartes himself. Stopping thinking in order to act doesn't mean despising reason; you're simply putting it in its place. We've talked about hypnosis, yoga, non-thinking, archery...Yet it was the inventor of modern rationalism who drew a distinction between thought and action with such exemplary firmness. When you're thinking, you have all the time in the world. You can shut yourself away for a week, meditate, write, dream, perhaps. There's no hurry. But as you learn in the second maxim of his *Discourse on the Method*, when life, with its demands, calls upon you—there's no time to lose. You must decide, most of the time with no real certainty. Descartes started out life as a soldier. He understood that it's less the content of a decision than the strength of your resolution that will either finish you off or get you out of trouble. The following episode was what convinced him.

Around 1621, aged twenty-five, Descartes left the army and traveled for pleasure. After a long journey, curiosity led him to visit East Frisia, in north Germany, so he hired a boat just for himself and his manservant. The "mariners" he took into his service, finding the Frenchman wealthy and inoffensive in appearance, decided to knock him senseless, rob him of everything he had, and throw him into the water. A stranger from a foreign land, he was known to no one, and no one was likely to miss him. They discussed all this out loud in front of the young man in question, never imagining for a moment that he might know any language other than his own. And what do you suppose our philosopher did? Did he, like a good rationalist, try to convince them it was a bad idea? To negotiate a deal in exchange for his life? To appeal to their religious feeling by reminding them of divine punishment? No, nothing of the sort. He who set such store by the power of demonstration decided this time to make a demonstration of power. At this point, there's no going back: he must succeed, or die. If they sensed the slightest wavering in him, he would have been done for. Adrien Baillet tells us:

> Monsieur Descartes, seeing that the moment had come, rose suddenly to his feet, with a greatly altered expression, drew his sword with unexpected pride, spoke to them in their language in a tone which at once caught their attention, and threatened to run them through that instant if they dared to insult him. It was during this encounter that he came to realize the impression that can be created by boldness that on other occasions might simply be seen as mere saber rattling. The impression he gave on this occasion had a most marvelous effect on the spirits of the wretched men. The horror it

inspired in them was followed by a sense of shock which prevented them from seizing their advantage and they treated him as delicately as he could possibly have wished.

Yes, the greatest philosopher of the modern era was also a man of action. A French knight first, thinker second.

8

Hit the Target
Without Aiming

I do not seek, I find

PICASSO

The first private lesson I ever gave was to Vanessa, a pupil in her final year of school. She had a 4 out of 20 in philosophy, and was due to sit her baccalaureate at the end of the year. I had never actually given any lessons before, but as a 21-year-old student trying to pay his rent, I had signed up to a list of students who were willing to give lessons, and then forgotten all about it. One day there was a message on my answering machine. It was Vanessa. We arranged to meet at her parents' house. Vanessa was very nice, if a little despairing of her situation—a 4, after all, is very far from being a 20—and visibly stressed by the prospect of the exam. I decided at once to share my secret weapon with her, the one I employed myself to get through school tests with relative ease.

"You know, Vanessa, certain goals can only be achieved indirectly. For example, if you think too hard about the bac and nothing else, on the day of the test you'll be paralyzed with fear. If you think too hard about a goal, you increase your chances of missing it. Here, make two balls of paper. Take the first one, aim carefully at the bin. When you're ready, throw it. Take your time. Really concentrate. Aim carefully. Missed! OK. Now, where did you last go on vacation? Was it nice? And where would you like to go next time?"

I wait for her to answer, then: "Now, don't think about it, take the second ball of paper and throw it in the bin. You see, this time you got it in. If you want to pass your bac, the best thing to do is not think about it."

"Maybe," Vanessa says, "but even so, I do have to do some work. I need at least to aim at the goal, don't I? Otherwise how am I going to get any better at philosophy?"

"Of course we're going to work. But not in order to pass the bac, just in order to have a better understanding. You know, Descartes didn't have the bac, nor did Plato—they just did philosophy for themselves, for pleasure and personal necessity. Not so they could take tests in it. What they invented is fascinating for its own sake. I suggest you forget about the bac, and just think about philosophy. If you're really interested in it, and start getting real pleasure out of it, you'll get your bac indirectly, without any effort and almost without thinking about it. I know it sounds paradoxical, but you saw what happened with the balls of paper. You don't hit the target by taking aim. When you think about it, in fact the opposite applies. If you're taking aim, then you're already thinking you might miss. Otherwise you wouldn't be taking aim. So aiming is already partly missing, or starting to miss. You won't progress by training yourself to aim, but rather by training yourself not to aim. Next time, I'll lend you a book by Alain, called *Minerve ou de la sagesse* (Minerva, or on Wisdom). Look at the chapter called "L'art de l'attention" (The Art of Attention), where he says you won't understand something by endlessly reading, taking notes, and shuffling papers. Getting agitated is not a good method for thinking: it's just like trying to hit the nail on the head a hundred times but missing by a fraction; actually hitting it on the head always happens the first time, and the key is not to try. Remember what Master Yoda tells Luke Skywalker in *Star Wars*: 'Don't try. Either do it or don't do it, but don't try.'"

"Can I really quote *Star Wars* in my test?" Vanessa asks in amazement. She must be starting to think I'm a fraud.

"No, don't do that. You can quote Alain. The important thing is to remember: some ends can only be achieved indirectly. If you really want to cite the author, it's Nietzsche who said that. The most important thing is to apply it. If you understand that philosophy is made to be put to the test and not just written about, you'll be home and dry. Safe from boredom, fear, and the frustration of not understanding. Ideas are tools that help us grasp reality. The more you understand, the happier you'll be. And it's a kind of happiness you can't lose: once you've understood something, it's forever. And while you're at it, you're likely to get higher marks. It's a device, a bit like the Trojan horse, but instead of being a mean trick to trap other people, it's a kindly trick, directed at yourself, that helps free you from worrying about failing."

"If I understand correctly," Vanessa says, "the less I think about the bac, the more chance I have of passing it. The less I think about what mark I get in philosophy, the more chance I have of getting a good mark. That seems a bit weird, don't you think? If you don't aim at something at all, how can you ever achieve it?"

"In fencing, they talk about those who use 'means' and those who use 'judgment.' The former aim for a goal and then use the means necessary to achieve it. The latter achieve their goal without even thinking about it. The first have technique, the second have intuition. They're two radically different approaches. Either you start with an intention, then reflect on how to put it into action, then do it. Or you marry the intention and the execution and the action works out without you thinking about it in advance. Obviously, the second approach is the winner, because it's always one step ahead, it's faster than thought. And a fencer who starts with the first approach can, as they get better at it, progress to the second one, and become increasingly intuitive. When we watch a great fencer, it looks natural—and it is. It's the same in everyday life. If someone *tries* to be natural, they can never do it. Awareness of their goal gets in the way. Which is why people who are hopelessly in love are always clumsy: they're so busy thinking about being natural, they become ridiculous. They think too hard about their goal and it paralyzes them."

"Like me with the bac."

"Exactly. You could call it the Cyrano syndrome. Cyrano de Bergerac, Edmond Rostand's famous character—played by Gérard Depardieu in the film—is a man of many gifts, but with a very large nose. You know the scene where he draws his sword to fight someone who's made fun of his nose: 'at the end of the *envoi* I'll touch him!' His virtuosity makes it possible for him both to aim, because he announces when he's going to prick his opponent, and to improvise a way of managing to do so, because he has to surprise his opponent. He multiplies the difficulty by improvising a poem in rhyming couplets as he fights (*envoi* has a dual meaning here; both 'duel,' and the final verse of a poem or ballad, typically a dedication). He fights as if the combat really didn't interest him. Which is why he wins. He reaches his goal while giving the impression of not even trying. This indifference to the goal is the great secret of all martial arts. To take aim is to court failure by considering failure even to be a possibility, rather as vertigo makes you more likely to fall by imagining it. If you aim for too long, you wear yourself out before you've fired your shot. Cyrano doesn't aim, he touches. At the first attempt. He doesn't try, he succeeds. Where does this effortlessness come from? It comes from his talent, obviously, but above all from his attitude. Superbly indifferent to success, untouched by fear, he seems to be above everything. 'But we don't fight in hope of winning! No! No, it's so much more beautiful when it's useless!' His famous panache is often wrongly mistaken for the showiness of losers. But it's not that. Cyrano, because he has panache, leads the life of the conqueror, precisely because he is indifferent to success. One evening he triumphs single-handedly over a hundred opponents. Because he is the only one of all of them who isn't afraid to lose his life. The true paradox of Cyrano, his 'syndrome,' is that his skill, whether with words or in combat, goes hand in hand with a hopelessness in love, a pathological shyness, due to the size of his nose, which stops him from declaring his love for Roxane. Everything comes easily to him, except what he really cares about. So the difficulty comes less from the action itself than from what is at stake. Whatever he does with no care for the outcome, without fear—fighting, writing verses—he succeeds at, precisely because he doesn't think about it. But if he cares too much about his goal, if he thinks about it, aims for it, he fails. This is the moral of Cyrano: if you want to hit the target, you have to not care too much about it."

"OK," Vanessa says, "but how do you practice not taking aim? In practical terms?"

"In practical terms, roll another paper ball. If you get what I've been saying, you understand that Cyrano fears rejection by Roxane. Fearless in the face of death, he trembles before the woman he loves. If he didn't love her, he could surely have her. It's what you might call the Valmont syndrome, the exact opposite of the Cyrano syndrome. Have you read *Dangerous Liaisons*?" Vanessa nods. "Well then you know that Valmont, the incorrigible seducer, has any woman he wants, and even some he doesn't want, precisely because he doesn't *really* want any of them. He only excels at seduction as long as he remains indifferent to his prey. Since he is not in love, he is never at a loss, he is never awkward or unhappy: he is always master of the situation because he doesn't undertake any personal risk. This gives him the assurance that makes him irresistible. Like an expert archer, he only releases his arrow once it has already hit the target. A cruel Cupid, devoid of all scruple—nothing daunts him. Is he happy? That's not the question. He enjoys serial conquests, but does not know love. Or to be more exact, *because* he doesn't know love. Until the day he meets the beautiful, innocent, virtuous Madame de Tourvel. His exact opposite: no ulterior motive, pure of soul, loyal, incapable of concealment. He instantly succumbs to her charm, precisely because she has no wish to seduce him. Her natural state is irresistible because it is sincere. This will be too much for Valmont. Of course, he will eventually get what he wants, and make her fall in love with him, but the rose has thorns: in the process he will fall in love with her. This will be both his salvation and his ruin. Incapable of sincere feeling, or of giving up his comfortable life as a heedless seducer, he literally dies from fear of loving her. When he cares too much about his target, he ends up like Cyrano. Now, throw your ball of paper into the bin. Don't think, don't aim."

"Darn, missed. I aimed again."

"So you did. Never mind. You get the idea. Like anything we really want, love is one of those ends that can only be achieved indirectly. It's like the song in *Carmen* says: 'Love is a rebellious bird that nobody can tame.' You can try to be nice but you have no control over whether you're loved. The only way to be happy in love is therefore to love without expecting anything back. You have a right to hope for it, but it's better to be happy just loving, or even better, to be happy, period. Love is a consequence of being happy to be alive, a bonus, the cherry on the cake. Romain Gary, the twentieth-century French novelist, says in *Gros-Câlin*: 'I know that reciprocal love exists, but I'm not aiming for luxury. Having someone to love is the first necessity.' You should never expect reciprocity, not as if you simply deserved it. It's only possible based on freedom. Nothing is less attractive than someone who's desperately trying to be lovable. The paradox, again, is that in order to be loved you need to not try."

"So what do you do?"

"Nothing. Just be satisfied with being. A tree is happy to give fruit, it doesn't care who eats it. You don't give presents in order to receive thanks, but rather for the pleasure of giving. It's better to stay true to yourself and not try to please others at any cost. Freedom and the form of supreme indifference that comes with it are again the better strategy, as they guarantee at least that one will stay true to oneself. Loving doesn't just mean loving someone, when the question of reciprocity is bound to arise, but also loving this or that, loving this activity, or that. Loving walking, or running, or swimming, or reading, or cooking, or looking, etc. Loving painting, music, nature. When you devote yourself entirely to what you love doing, your love overwhelms any awareness of outside approval, or of your ultimate goal, and you're bound to do it better. And oddly, it's when you're completely caught up in something that you're at your most lovable. You see the paradox: being absorbed in what you're doing to the point where you forget everything, loving what you do with a passion, also makes you both as effective and as lovable as it's possible to be. It's just at the point when you forget who you are, the moment when you feel you're no one at all, that you're most yourself."

"Another case of when you're not aiming for the goal you hit it…"

"Exactly. And in love it's even more striking because the 'target,' when it knows it's being aimed at, is bound to act differently. If you care too much about the target, they sense it."

"But if you don't care about it enough, it's no better."

"You might agree with Sartre—in his view, love means being the victim of a fundamental contradiction: when I love, I want the other to be free, I want him to love me freely, but at the same time, I want him to love only me, I want his freedom to be reduced to just loving me."

"It's a vicious circle."

"There's no way out. The lover always plays a big part in love, feeding it with his or her imagination. Stendhal defines 'crystallization' in love as 'the operation of the spirit, which takes everything as a revelation of new perfections in the beloved.' In other words, to love is to invent qualities in the person one loves, and to believe they possess them for real. Love is creation."

"Does that mean it is an illusion?"

"Yes and no. Let's just say that in love, the 'work' does itself. When all is said and done, there's nothing you can do, you just have to be. No need to aim. If you haven't already hit the target there's no point in trying."

"That's why Cupid is always shown with a bow!"

"Well spotted! Willpower is useless in love. Feelings can't be forced. So there's no point in getting worked up about it. When it comes to it, the thing's already settled. It's true of friendship too. Why are we friends with someone? Montaigne says, referring to his friend Étienne de La Boétie: 'Because it was him, because it was me. We were looking for each other before we ever met...by some heavenly decree, I believe.' No effort is required, in friendship or in love. No need for feats; merit doesn't come into it. Either it flows or it doesn't, like an electric current. I'm talking about the beginning, obviously. Afterward, it's more like the electrical grid: you do need to look after it a bit."

"I get it. But it's always the same," Vanessa says. "When I understand something, I can't explain it afterward. It's easy when I think about it, and difficult when I have to write it down."

"That's the same for everyone. You just have to write as if you were talking to someone. There's nothing to stop you writing your essay like a letter, and that's what it is, in the end, since someone's going to read it. It's almost a love letter: love for philosophy, to be shared with someone. This is what 'philo-sophy' means, after all: love for wisdom, or the wisdom of love. Out of the hundreds of exam papers a teacher has to read when they're marking the bac, if there's one that feels as though it's really addressed to them, it will have an effect. The chances are they'll feel more involved, more interested. Choose a real person, or a made-up person in your head, and write to them to explain something. Imagine their objections and reply to them, construct a real dialogue. Even Descartes is much easier to follow and more enjoyable to read when he's writing to Princess Elisabeth of Bohemia—they had a fascinating and eloquent correspondence. Philosophy is difficult when it's just ideas floating around; it's much easier when it's *for* someone. Plato dramatizes Socrates in his *Dialogues*, where he spends the whole time clashing with his opponents. When two people are arguing in front of a witness, it's immediately more exciting than when you lay out abstract arguments. *Gorgias*, a conversation between Socrates and a group of supporters of Gorgias, is like a heavyweight boxing match: Gorgias in one corner, champion of the sophists, and Socrates in the other, champion of the philosophers. You can write imagining that you can hear a conversation, for example, between yourself and your brother, or between you and me. When you don't think about the words you're using, just about the person you're writing to, it comes naturally. Some aims can only be reached..."

"...Indirectly."

"Exactly."

"But I don't know *how* to write."

"Did you ever play cops and robbers when you were little, or doctors, or superheroes, or at being a pop star? On the playground, everyone makes believe. But even as an adult, if you make believe, it can work. Have you had any driving lessons? If you pretend to know, if you act as though you already knew, it will give you the confidence you need to drive for real. When you do something for the first time, the knack is to do it as though you already knew how. You mustn't go on and on thinking about it, you just have to get on with it. With blind confidence. Remember? You either do it or you don't but you mustn't try."

"How can you try to not try?"

"The key is in your attitude. Sit up straight. Express your pride through your posture. If you hold yourself proudly, you will be proud of what you do. Pretend to be proud, mime being proud, and you will end up feeling it for real. You have to go through your body if you want to change your soul. Descartes explains it in his *Traité des passions* (Treaty of the Passions). Directly, there's nothing you can do about the feelings that possess you. Sadness, for example. You can't get rid of it by an act of will. There's nothing worse than when someone says: 'But you have every reason in the world to be happy! You've no right to be sad.' If you've no reason to be sad, it makes you even sadder. It's a spiral. Descartes recommends something different: to think about a time when you've felt joy and mime that joy—that is to say, put your body in the same situation or the same position. The last time I felt happy, I was whistling such and such a tune. I was standing tall and walking briskly, breathing freely. Well then—how would it be if instead of staying slumped on the sofa feeling depressed I got up, walked around, stood tall, and breathed freely while whistling my favorite tune? The knack is to go via your body rather than force it through your will. If I put my body back in a state of joy, my mind will really feel the joy I start by miming. What is difficult or impossible when you approach it through the will is easy via the body. Another example—I can see you're scared to death of failing your bac..."

"I'm not scared."

"It's just an example. So, if you want to get rid of your fear, wanting alone won't do it! Willing and thinking have no direct effect against fear. Which is why, despite all the things I'm telling you, you're still scared to death."

"No I'm not!"

"Yes you are. Your will is powerless. You can't change your mood just by making a decision. You're going to have to find a trick, a way around. Go via your body rather than your mind. What will you say to your children the day they have to take their bac? That you didn't go because you were scared witless?"

"Stop it, I am going to go!"

"Of course you are, and it's going to be fine. Do you know why? Because you've stopped being scared. Now you're angry. Do you see the trick? You can't get rid of your fear by thinking about it, but by instead feeling anger or shame, for example. By playing one passionate feeling against another. In other words, thinking about it won't change a strong feeling, but another strong feeling will. If you manage to make someone who's frightened angry, they'll forget they were frightened. And you have to learn to do it by yourself. John McEnroe, a great tennis champion, knew how to make himself angry just at the right moment: when he was beginning to have doubts, and starting to feel the game slip away from him, he used anger as a yogi uses meditation: to refocus himself. To stop other emotions from destabilizing him. To destabilize his opponent too, of course, but above all to sharpen his own concentration and think about nothing other than the game. Paradoxically, the angrier McEnroe got, the calmer he became. Shame can restore people's courage too. That's why I mentioned your future children. And love is even more effective. That's Yannick Noah's technique, as team captain. He gives his players enough love to be able to fight back fear, whether of losing or of winning. If I do something for love, I do it better than if I was just doing it for myself. 'You're not alone, we love you, even if you lose' is more effective than 'You're on your own, we'll only love you if you win.' While we're on the subject of fear, I'll tell you one more thing: fear comes from your imagination. So you just have to keep your mind busy with something else and stop it thinking about what it's afraid of. You need to find it something to do that's hard enough for it to have to pay attention—but not too hard. It has to be something you know how to do. It might just be watching a good TV series. I say 'good' because otherwise your mind wanders off to something else. Concentrating on your breathing, if that's all there is, always works. Observing a slow, deep rhythm, in time to an imaginary metronome, which brings back calm and a regular pulse. Do you see? Instead of confronting fear directly you must banish it indirectly."

"Without taking aim. I get it."

"Feeling better?"

"It worked. I'm not scared now."

"Are you angry?"

"A bit. For being so stupid, mostly."

"Well, stop that. Or I'll start getting cross. How do you know you're stupid?"

"Well...It speaks for itself, doesn't it? It's written on my work, in black and white. The teacher even gave me some extra work, and though she didn't use the word, it felt like a punishment. I had to write four pages on the subject: 'Does work make you free?'"

"That reminds me of something. Show me your essay...'Insufficient work, blah blah, lack of discipline, blah blah, more effort required with expression.' Lots of red, not much support. It's more like something you'd write on a school report than a comment on a piece of work, a correction. Or else it's a correction in the worst sense of the word, like 'correcting' offenders. Do you know where the word 'discipline' comes from? It has two meanings, which eventually became entangled with each other. To start with, in classical Latin, the disciple is someone who learns—*discere* meaning 'to learn.' A discipline is a science, or a branch of knowledge. A few centuries later, in church Latin, the word acquired the meaning of correction, punishment, the monastic rule. Discipline was no longer something you learned, but the means of learning it, of getting it into your head, using a 'rule,' and where necessary, a ruler, or a whip: the word 'discipline' ended up, in the Middle Ages, meaning the whip used for flagellation, and can even be used in the sense of 'carnage' or 'massacre,' the outcome of meting out justice. The idea that justice might lead to a massacre itself teaches us a great deal about the mentality of the era. In a few centuries, we thus went from the ancient world's view, in which punishment is reserved for those who don't work, to the Christian vision, in which punishment has become both the rule, the means, and, in actual fact, the sole content of teaching. *Suffer, you must suffer*—there will always be something of that. As when people say: 'That will teach you!' God has punished us. Suffering is not an accident, it's a destiny, the consequence of original sin. To exist is to be guilty and we must pay. Punishment is no longer a last resort when there's no better option and patience has worn thin—it becomes an end in itself. You will be born in pain and through pain you will learn. There is no other route but that of the cross and suffering. As though the only worthwhile imitation of Christ was of his final hours. School is always organized on this assumption, and punishment, where it exists, usually consists of the imposition of extra work. Setting a task by way of punishment means recognizing the equivalence of work and punishment, and that school itself is just one long chastisement, fortunately punctuated with play breaks and holidays. Most people, when asked, speak of school as an ordeal. Whereas if you examine the words, 'educate,' from the Latin *exducere*, means literally 'to lead out of.' The French word *'connaître,'* 'to know,' literally means to 'be born with' ('co' comes from *cum* in Latin—'with': we grow thanks to what we learn). *'Apprendre,'* 'to learn,' means to take from the outside, as in 'apprehend,' in English (Latin prefix *ad*, 'toward'). What is apparent in these words is the movement toward the exterior. To be born, *'naître,'* may be painful in passing, but this pain is not the goal of birth; it is the inevitable consequence of our passage from inside to outside. A baby cries not from the horror of its descent into incarnation, but from the pain of its lungs opening like flowers, its eyes passing from darkness to light, its skin leaving the gentle balm of liquid and meeting the stinging air; it's a passing pain that will soon become a pleasure, a joy: the joy of existing. Ex-ist, *ex-stare*, to stand outside oneself. To pass from the interior to the exterior, leaving the mother's womb to enter the world. Its eyes will soon have something to see, its skin something to feel, the body something to do. Growth itself can cause pain or difficulty, but pain is not the purpose of growth; it is sometimes its corollary. For the Greeks, and for Aristotle in particular, the purpose of growth is the passing from the potential to the act. Potential is the possibility enclosed within each person, what they may become. An act is potential realized, become effective. As a seed becomes a plant, a flower, and then a fruit. The fruit was held in potential inside the seed; the fruit is the seed as act. This passing from inside to outside is an expression—a pressing-out: something is pressing, pushing from inside toward the outside, in order to be fulfilled. This is a natural movement; you don't have to suffer to grow. Or more exactly, if there is suffering, it's just growing pains, linked to an increase in potential, an unfolding of one's being as it reaches its true dimensions. These pains are never inflicted from the outside. You don't pull on leaves or on the roots of a tree to make it grow. The tree itself stretches its leaves toward the sun and its roots down toward water. The effort it makes is an effort it *is*, and which costs it nothing. It's the tree that wants to grow, to fulfill its purpose.

"But fulfilling one's purpose, as a human being, means leaving the animal state behind. A child doesn't grow like a plant, doesn't get bigger like an animal, content to remain identical in every detail, repeating the law of the species over and over. To become human is to become—to turn into—someone. So you have to pull yourself clear of nature to become someone. Wrestle with what you were at birth, with nature, with instinct, in order to construct your humanity. This is the true sense of the word 'education': its purpose is to lead the child out of the semi-vegetative immediacy of its animal existence, to give it a human form, through the learning of language, the arts, sciences. The child will have to work. 'Man is formed through struggle,' Alain says; 'his true pleasures must be won, must be deserved. He must give before he receives. That is the law.'

"But the word 'work' has suffered the same fate as the word 'discipline.' According to a dubious but now commonly accepted etymology, '*travail*,' which means 'work' in French, comes from the word *tripalium*, an instrument of torture. Work means first of all the action of the executioner, whose job is to torture, to '*travail*' the condemned man. In English too, 'to work someone over' is to attack or injure them. Work, whether you are the subject or the object, consists of inflicting or receiving pain. But there are other etymological explanations, far more convincing and less violent ones. In '*travail*,' we find the prefix 'trans,' which means 'through' and suggests the idea of passage: '*travail*' transforms, allows the passage from one form to another. In '*travail*' we detect the English 'travel'; '*travail*,' rather than an effort in one place, stripped of its meaning and attached to its instrument of torture, describes an experience, a movement, a discovery: the forming of a new thing. '*Travail*,' like a journey, forms by transforming, shapes the world as well as the person passing through it. The word '*travail*,' heard correctly, ceases to be synonymous with suffering and penitence and promises instead fulfillment and pleasure.

"Over the course of a few centuries, we went from an idea of education founded on the expression of nature to a conception based on punishment. And if education is often experienced as a punishment, that is because, unfortunately, many teachers, and a good number of parents, who experienced the same system themselves, continue to consider and practice it as such. And yet threats never taught anyone anything. At best they teach people servile obedience, parroting the teacher's words, like wearing a dog collar when what you need is the freedom of wolves. Fear of punishment never generated a single original thought. The opposite would really be a miracle. Education is not rearing or raising. According to Rousseau, an early training in politeness can even be detrimental to the development of real virtue, by teaching us from a young age that it's enough just to say the right words, like magic spells, to get what we want. Paradoxically, politeness can create little tyrants. And when discipline is applied too young it may give adults some satisfaction but is quite unsuitable for the children themselves. Punishment is not only ineffective, it is counterproductive. Threats don't make people more confident or bolder: they make them fearful or indifferent. Anyone who believes that respect is learned through fear must have a very shoddy notion of respect: they're confusing it with obedience. When you're afraid, you learn nothing, you tremble. Look, pass me your sheet of paper, we're going to do a magic trick. Now scrunch it up into a ball. Go on. What have you got to lose? You really want to keep it? With a mark like that you're hardly going to frame it."

After a good few seconds' hesitation, Vanessa makes up her mind and crumples up her paper with some relish.

"There you go. Now you know what you have to do."

After a brief moment of reflection, just long enough to shut down all reflection, she sends the enormous ball of paper flying toward the bin, without aiming, or trembling. Just as she celebrates her perfect shot with a joyous shout of laughter and a "Yes!," *tap tap*, her mother knocks at the door. We hadn't noticed the time. Two hours had turned into three. Slightly taken aback, but exquisitely polite, the mother thanks me, hoping that her daughter's good humor indicates her reconciliation with philosophy, and that the results will follow. I hope so too, and I stand up before she notices the scrunched-up paper in the bin, clear proof that you can transform failure into success, and learn to hit your mark without aiming. Somewhat embarrassed, I take the envelope she offers, and slip it into my back pocket. Bye then, thank you. See you soon, perhaps. My turn now to do a magic trick: I vanish.

Pleased with this first experience, I walked back to the apartment where I was staying with my friend Sarah, in the busy Les Halles district. Determined to spend my newfound wealth, I invited her out to dinner. Night had fallen. We were walking down the Rue Montorgueil, the same street I had come home by, looking for a restaurant. Mechanically, I slipped my hand into my back pocket, only to find that it was empty. The envelope had disappeared. It was strange, I didn't really like the idea of being given money for the lesson: there must have been a kind of natural justice at work here. My pocket had made a Freudian slip and lost the money I didn't want. "Hang on," Sarah said, "let's look for it. Let's retrace your route." "There's no point, it was an hour ago, it's hopeless," I said. "Besides, I've spent all afternoon saying that there are certain goals that can only be achieved if you don't aim for them. So, if there's any truth in what I told my pupil, if I want to have even a tiny chance of finding this envelope, the one thing I mustn't do is look for it." Then, there, right in front of us, on the ground, in the middle of the pedestrian street, soiled by the shoes of heedless passersby, in the very spot where I had vowed not to look for it, was my envelope. With an uncanny feeling, I stooped down to pick it up, and opened it: the money was still inside. "You're kidding me," Sarah said, her eyes wide and disbelieving. "You knew it was there! It's impossible! How did you do it?" I hadn't done anything, obviously, but I've never forgotten the amazing feeling of losing and finding that envelope, against all odds, that little miracle, proving so irrefutably the truth of a principle that is at the heart of the book I'm now writing: certain goals can only be achieved if we don't aim at them. When I told my pupil Vanessa about it, at the next lesson, she found it incredible. But above all, if it worked for me, that meant it could work for her.

In the philosophy paper for the bac, a few months later, she got an 18. Better than I had done at her age. Certain goals can only be achieved indirectly. As they say at the end of a math proof: QED.

9

The Secret Laws of Attention

They don't see, because they're looking too hard

ALAIN

I'm writing this book by the sea. Rocked by the regular sound of the waves. Even when the sea isn't there, I imagine it in order to write. The sea is humanity's greatest secret, a secret we are only ever on the brink of understanding, even though it is spread out right before our eyes. But all we need to do is pay attention. Rhythm; the great secret is its rhythm. We think of the sea as a space, but above all it is time, circular time. The trough of the wave will also become its summit, sometime later, in a moment. And the summit will become a trough. The same point will be the lowest and the highest. Every high will become a low—humility—and every low will become a high—hope. It's both metaphor and reality. The sea exists, and what does its silence say? The philosopher Simone Weil wrote: "Every visible and palpable force is subject to an invisible limit that it will never exceed. In the sea, a wave rises up and up and up; but a certain point, even though there is nothing there but emptiness, stops it and makes it come back down." These words, written in 1943 in London, resonate like a promise. However high Hitler rises, he will in the end come down again: it's the rule of the waves and the rule of history. No progress is infinite; there is always a breaking point, a point of equilibrium. But the sea doesn't just teach us history lessons, it also offers us a most beautiful exercise in perception. In *Entretiens au bord de la mer* (Conversations by the Sea), Alain, who was Simone Weil's teacher, thinks of the ocean as a "breaker of idols": "The whole sea endlessly expresses the idea that forms are false. Nature in this fluid state rejects all our ideas." It is we who invent ideas, and then try to tack them onto the formless world. The sea doesn't think, it's happy just to be—everything changes there, nothing lasts. But it respects a rhythm. The wave breaks, then withdraws before returning; it draws its strength from this withdrawal that gives it momentum. The sea tells us that you have to learn to relax into effort, just as oarsmen know how to rest between each stroke. If you truly wish to act you must learn not to be always acting: rest must be integrated into the action. In *Minerva, or on Wisdom*, Alain notes: "If you're always holding on tight you'll hold badly. The true athlete relaxes during the game and only tightens their grip at the moment of contact."

The game is the one you're playing, and above all it's the game of your own body, of the muscles, the legs, the alternation of contraction and relaxation that is essential to effective action. Watch a sprinter in slow motion: you will see that their face is relaxed and their cheeks are without tension. The sprinter's aim, particularly in the last part of their race, is total relaxation. This law of alternation between effort and rest, embodied in the play of the sea's waves, is the first law of nature. This rhythm controls our whole life and it is better if we know it. Alain: "If you deprive yourself of sleep, you deprive yourself of waking. Someone who doesn't sleep enough is literally poisoned by his own restlessness. Someone who has slept is washed clean." Rest allows the mind to be cleansed and to renew itself like a wave. And we shouldn't think of this rest simply as night as opposed to day or as sleep opposed to waking: "Those who have carefully studied the faintest sounds have discovered something they were not looking for. A very faint, sustained sound is heard as intermittent. Our attention beats, like our pulse, it takes little naps, it backs off and then tunes back in." Contrary to general opinion, attention is never continuous. It's not a question of will, it cannot be so. It obeys a rhythm, it has highs and lows. Attention is a wave on which we must learn to surf.

In this chapter I have brought together everything required for an understanding of the mechanisms of our attention. It is a veritable recipe book and that is what I intended, so that you can come back to dip into it as you wish. I have called it "The

Secret Laws of Attention," because these laws, although they structure all our activities, remain essentially hidden. Facility is not a dream. It is within our grasp. We can begin at once—we just need to follow the right method.

Descartes' method

The point of a method, as its name suggests, is to make life easier. *Odos* or *hodos*, in Greek, means "the road." Descartes' method is one that shows which road to follow in order to think as easily as possible, but, as we shall see, it can also be used to guide our actions. It only has four rules: the (self-)evident; dividing up the difficulties; order; and enumeration.

1. The evident comes from the Latin *video*, "to see." The evident is what happens when you see something with the mind's eye, i.e., you understand it. The evident is not a starting point but a result. It is the result of attention. Imagine attention as a swath of light, the beam of a torch. This swath of light is narrow but intense. The attention cannot therefore shine on many objects at the same time. Ideally, attention should focus on only one point at a time. Therefore you must always:

2. Divide up the difficulties. Think of one thing at a time. Don't try to grasp everything at once. Don't be in a rush, take one step at a time, and take all the time you need to grasp what is evident in each part. Something that is particularly complex has to be

cut up into as many small parts as necessary. Once they are cut up and understood they must be put into:

3. Order. Thinking is putting the parts that one has cut up into the right order. This order is not natural, it is an intellectual order. A logical order and one that is invented, that of a mathematical proof, for example, or of a book or a manual for learning how to play tennis. You go from the simple toward the complex so as to progress from the easiest to the most difficult. It is order that makes this progress easy. Since you have cut up the complexity into little parts and have put them in a new order, you then have to be sure that you haven't forgotten anything and therefore proceed to an:

4. Enumeration. A naming of parts. An overview. A panorama. Call it what you will, the idea is to be certain that you have not left out an important part. The risk, when you bring your attention to bear on one point, is that you lose sight of the bigger picture. You must therefore regularly widen your point of view to make sure that everything is included.

OK. Now that I have introduced you to the four rules of the Cartesian method, all of which rest on the observation that our attention is narrow, and cannot take many things in at the same time, nor understand them quickly, I should add that attention doesn't last very long either. Therefore you must above all be able to rest, to relax completely between two moments of concentration and learn to know yourself well enough to see how long you can concentrate without faltering. For Montaigne it was ten minutes. Paying attention means not trying or tensing up. You must never, ever insist. Montaigne: "What I don't see at the first shot, I see even less when I keep on trying." You don't keep on trying, you relax, try again later when you've recovered a little. That might be after a few seconds. Or several minutes. Or the next day. To each his own rhythm.

The essential point is never to try to overcome complexity in one go. Not to try to understand everything, nor understand it all at once. To resolve a problem, you must dissolve it, and divide into as many parts as possible what at first sight seems like an overwhelming mass. If you observe this method, provided that you divide up the difficulties, then organize them in order of difficulty "to advance little by little, by degrees," like the steps of a staircase, as Descartes says, it doesn't matter what the object of your thought is, "there cannot be anything so distant that you won't reach it, or so hidden that you won't discover it." Just take one step at a time, don't dash off down the line of proof, any more than the tightrope walker runs along his rope: he only takes the next step if he is balanced. This way you will go as far as it is possible to go.

This rule of dividing up difficulty and concentrating effort also works with action. Alain: "Don't do all the action in one go; don't get ready to take a single leap over the hill; don't think of all those miles still to go." Napoleon, in a very Cartesian way, recommends that one should not attack everywhere at the same time. It is better to restrict oneself to precise places, and bring all one's attention to bear on them. An action of maximum intensity aimed at a single place will be more effective than an effort that is dispersed. Dividing up the difficulty does not mean dividing up your effort; it means concentrating your effort on one point, then another. Napoleon engaged not in "parallel warfare" of old-fashioned strategy, in which you fought everywhere at the same time, but rather in warfare of maneuver, which consists of attacking certain strategic points with all one's strength. Rather than fighting in a line, you drive nails into the joints and vital organs of the enemy. Acupuncture proceeds in much the same way: you have a greater effect by placing a few needles carefully on precise spots than by spreading them all over the surface of the body. This entails knowing where exactly to place them. Therefore you must simplify your vision, not get lost in the details, and always keep an overview. "There are many good generals in Europe," said Napoleon, "but they see too many things; I see the big shapes and attack them, certain that the peripheral ones will then collapse of their own accord." If one attacks the complexities in the right order, some will disappear of their own accord. This question of order also concerns the organization of the attack: "One does not win a war with a large number of troops, but with well-organized and disciplined troops." It's not that things are easy or difficult. It is the order you put them in that creates ease. Order, and the place where you attack.

Plato and the art of cutting up a chicken

Plato compared dialectic, or the art of thinking clearly, to cutting up a chicken: you mustn't force it, by going straight at the bone, but rather slip the knife in at the point of least resistance, at the joint between the bones. Thinking clearly is separating what is already distinct, respecting the anatomy of things simply by being attentive to them. You don't cut roughly, you slip in subtly, looking for the joint. The blade of the mind destroys nothing, but slips in between the ideas. Understanding a problem is the same thing as understanding a chicken. Vegetarians probably won't like this metaphor, but you can adapt it to fruit and vegetables. There is an art to separating a fruit from its skin without damaging it, in slipping your nail and then your finger between the orange and its peel to separate them without spilling juice, to peeling a banana without crushing it, to cutting a peach without jabbing the stone. The metaphor loses a little of its toughness; in the absence of bones you can actually cut a fruit or a vegetable any way you like, but it is improved on a different level, since it assumes a more careful attention to subtle resistances, and introduces the idea of time and ripening. You can judge the ripeness of an avocado from the way that its flesh adheres, or doesn't, to the stone, but by then it is too late to close it up again. It is better, before opening it, to judge it like a peach or an apricot from the firmness of its flesh. But in the case of the avocado, the thickness of the skin makes this examination less than certain. As in the case of melons, you can look to see whether the stem or stalk is beginning to come away. In all cases, touch and observation are far better than the knife. The hand feels and knows that where there is a resistance it is not yet ripe. You have to be able to wait. When it's ripe it's obvious. Here you have both a principle of thought and of action: if you look for the joints and apply your effort there, there will actually be no need for effort. Paying attention is like slipping between things where it is easy, rather than attacking them any old way.

The Orpheus syndrome, or the law of inverted effort

Why did Orpheus turn back to look at Eurydice? Obviously because he had been forbidden to do so. It's not really Orpheus who is responsible for the second death of his wife, but the perverse Hades, god of the infernal regions, who trapped him in the simplest way: by putting into his mind the thought of the forbidden action. The god of the infernal regions sows the seed of evil and invents temptation. If Orpheus hadn't been thinking about not turning back to see Eurydice, he would not have done it. When you think you are resisting a temptation, you are already imagining yielding to it. Because in making an effort to oppose a thought, one strengthens the thought. One could call that the Orpheus syndrome, or the law of inverted effort.

"There comes a moment," writes the Christian philosopher Jean Guitton, in *Le travail intellectuel* (Intellectual Work), "when the effort brought to bear on an external obstacle produces an internal obstacle that is more insidious than the other and constantly increases it, the more so if you struggle against it, as can be seen with people who stammer." When you struggle against a forbidden image,

> a certain way of directing your effort in order to banish the image makes it more likely you will intensify it. The body cannot tell the difference between no and yes. To say "I am not afraid, I do not wish to be afraid of this passing shell," means amplifying the images you are trying to resist. By trying not to tremble at moments of fear, you simply increase the trembling. Tensing up so as not to yield to temptation makes you likely to give in to it more quickly. Old Coué said, in—to my view—overly geometric language, that when there is a struggle between the imagination and the will, the imagination will expand to equal the square of the will. The law of the inversion of misdirected effort is one of the most profound laws of our psyche. I am amazed people don't talk about it more and that it isn't taught. Whenever, in spite of excellent guides and sincere good intentions, I have failed to learn a simple art (geometry, or riding, for instance), it is because my teachers were unaware of this principle of inversion. I would stiffen on the horse's back, as before a theorem, and the result was either that I fell, or was plunged into darkness. You must work in a state of relaxation. True attention comes from trying not to try. You must avoid this

inversion of effort, which is fatal in almost every case of prolonged tension. The art of not even trying consists in never allowing one's will to become irritated and to tense up; in imitating natural creatures; in letting oneself go; in "humoring one's will," as Montaigne says; that is to say, never willing something unless consciously and at the right moment, remembering that the will, as a life force, can also grow weary and lose focus. There is a state of abandoned thought, somewhat mindless, a semi-waking dream which favors memory, invention and also writing.

Simone Weil and attention as negative effort

So, Simone Weil was a pupil of Alain. He said of her that she was capable of truly understanding Spinoza, which is no small compliment, since he said it of only two people, her and... Goethe. Spinoza affirmed that "what is beautiful is rare and difficult" and distinguished three types of knowledge: the first type, which consists merely of lining up facts that one cannot verify, known only by hearsay (my date of birth, for example) and off-the-cuff judgments made by the imagination (the moon must be a few hundred meters away, it looks so close tonight); the second type, which produces truths by employing the difficult and roundabout route of rational proofs (mathematics, philosophy); and finally, the third type, which has the same content as that of the second type, but gets there more directly, by intuition, with ease, and in which, Spinoza promises, we experience a sense of eternity in this life "as far as that is possible." At the end of the difficult road of reason shines the "love of God"—intuitive understanding, in other words—with no effort on one's own part, or that of others, or of nature. How do you reach this light? You must work, you must go through all the rigors of proof. It's beautiful, and therefore "rare and difficult," but strangely—and this is my point—the battle of the truth against what is false requires no tension, no effort against oneself. The spirit must simply obey its own nature, which is to think of what is true in order to triumph over what is false, indirectly, exactly as the day, when it breaks, triumphs over the darkness without resistance or struggle. The spirit's perfect nature is to understand: the more it understands, the greater its joy. When I think, therefore I am not making an effort against myself, I am simply persisting in being what I am. I am trying to be ever more what I already am. I don't make an effort, I *am* the effort—as Spinoza says, a *conatus* (from the Latin *conari*: "to try, to strive for")—which costs me nothing since I am simply doing what comes most naturally to me. To put it another way, anyone who makes an effort to understand will never understand. That's not how it works.

Understanding can't be forced. At most, it can be prepared for. When we understand, there is no tension. It's more like a kind of light.

And that's where Simone Weil comes in. In a text called *Attente de Dieu* (Waiting for God), a title that clearly indicates its Christian orientation, Simone Weil draws our attention to a truth about our minds that is as valid on a cognitive level as on a spiritual one: paying attention is not what we think. I have decided to quote generously from this book because it is unrivaled in its perfection and its simplicity and because its truth, as Simone Weil indicates at the end of the text, is relevant not only to believers.

Most often, attention is confused with some kind of muscular effort. If you say to pupils: "Now pay attention," you see them frown, hold their breath, tense their muscles. If, after two minutes, you ask them what they have been paying attention to, they can't give you an answer. They haven't being paying attention to anything. They haven't been paying attention. They've been tensing their muscles. In studying you often expend this kind of muscular effort. As it ends up being tiring, you feel as though you've been working. This is an illusion. Tiredness has no relationship with work. This kind of muscular effort when studying is completely sterile, even when carried out with the best of intentions.

[...] Intelligence can only be led by desire. For desire to exist there must be pleasure and joy. Intelligence only grows and bears fruit in joy. The joy of learning is as essential to study as breathing is to runners.

Attention is an effort, the greatest effort of all, perhaps, but it is a negative effort. In itself it does not entail tiredness. When tiredness is felt attention is almost impossible unless you are well practiced; so then it is better to give in, look for some relaxation and begin again a bit later, letting yourself go and bringing yourself back, just as you breathe in and out.

Twenty minutes of intense attention without any tiredness is infinitely more valuable than that kind of application with furrowed brow which says "I've worked hard," with a sense of duty done.

[...]

[When you get it wrong], it's almost always because you tried to be active; you tried to seek. The most precious things must not be sought, but waited for. There is for every schoolbook exercise a specific way of waiting for truth "desirefully," without going out to look for it. Of paying attention to the details of a geometrical problem without looking for the solution; a way of paying attention to the words of a Latin or Greek text without looking for the meaning; of waiting, when one is writing, for the right word to flow from your pen of its own accord.

[...] For any adolescent who can grasp this truth and is generous enough to desire this fruit above all others, studying will have a full and rich spiritual impact even where there is no framework of religious belief.

Attention is therefore a negative effort, in the sense that it costs nothing, calls for no expenditure of energy, and produces no tiredness. If you feel tired when you are paying attention, it is because you are tensing up unnecessarily; you are mistakenly making an effort, instead of letting things come to you. Attention is a pure gaze, incompatible with tiredness. Alain states: "Before the war, I often used to get hooked on a problem and would struggle thinking about it without making any progress. That is the same mistake as staring at something one wants to see properly. Often I have encountered these insistent gazes, applied to the quest for knowledge; they don't see, because they are looking too hard." Attention must be as easy and relaxed as a well-trained athlete and the first condition for it is rest. Attention obeys the primordial rhythm of the breath or the sea. Studying is therefore worth nothing in and of itself, the grades are worthless (Alain's best pupil tells us that), and the principal value of geometry and poetry lies in the fact that they provide training in a certain kind of attention. Why? Because if I am truly capable of attention, then one day I will be in a position to pay attention to other people. I will be incapable of *not* seeing them. And seeing properly is already a way of doing good. A universal spiritual truth, says Simone Weil, that concerns not only believers, but all human beings.

Working with Sartre in the café

Jean-Paul Sartre was also one of Alain's pupils. He doesn't talk about Alain, or only very little, but Sartre agrees with Alain and Simone Weil at least on the question of attention, in that it should not be an effort. In one of his most famous texts, *L'Être et le néant* (Being and Nothingness), on *mauvaise foi* (bad faith), he writes: "The attentive pupil who wants to be attentive, his eye fixed on the teacher, ears wide open, wears himself out so much by playing the attentive one that he ends up not listening at all." Believing that attention is an effort is exhausting. And pretending to be attentive to please the teacher prevents you from understanding. Here we find again the law of the inversion of misdirected effort: the harder one pushes oneself toward a goal, the more likely one is to miss it.

Sartre, who wrote this text in the middle of the ordered chaos of the Café de Flore, is clearly suggesting that the peace and quiet of a classroom is perhaps less favorable to understanding and intellectual work than the relative disorder of a café. In the café, attention seems blocked from the very first moment, condemned to be dispersed. Yet certain people manage to work there, Sartre being one of them, and indeed some people can only work there, amid the noise of others and the hubbub of life. Silence is not always favorable. When the attention is distracted, it grasps the truth out of the corner of its eye as it passes, like a skillful fisherman. Such distraction sometimes provides the solution to a problem you can't resolve by tackling it head-on. Some distracting activity can therefore actually make work easier. It enables you not to think of what you are doing and to be content with simply doing it.

It also builds up momentum. When you are in a busy environment you avoid the difficulty of beginning, and you understand that the only thing to do is to carry on. Some people like working to music. I am one of them. Music always draws us in, taking us by the hand, and we take advantage of its movement.

Running to music also has its devotees: you run better, farther, more easily; you forget the effort. Attention, caught up by the music, allows the body to do what comes naturally without getting tangled up in thought.

Scrub the pan or let it soak

Let's return to the example of the pan, the one we burned in the introduction to this book. It is quite clear that there are two different ways to clean it—to scrub or not to scrub, that is the question. Either one scrubs with all one's might, and it's hard work, or one leaves it to soak and allows water and time to do their work—the crafty way. The first method is based on effort, the second on ease. Effort saves time and wastes energy (and incidentally runs the risk of damaging the pan). The second method, which is easier, requires time, and saves time, since in the end cleaning the pan after having soaked it will be quicker and require much less effort. You'll have less work to do, and you'll do it better. Postponing the action and letting things look after themselves is a win-win, because the result is better from every point of view. Far from giving in to ease out of laziness, you have demonstrated ingenuity in finding a simpler and more effective approach. You've chosen patience. This second solution is at once more rational and more economical: in a nutshell, more elegant. Speaking of elegance when you're washing the dishes might seem exaggerated or out of place, but elegance is linked to the idea of economy and rationality. Whether in fashion, in science, or in everyday life, the most elegant solution is always the most economical one. Descartes and Coco Chanel would agree on that. A little black dress, like a mathematical proof, aims at understatement, simplicity. Nothing chichi, no useless ornaments—that's the way to go. That's what beauty is. But watch out, for sometimes the most effective solution is precisely not to wait, but to leap straight into action. For example, to stick with dishwashing, it's better to clean a dish in which you have cooked a duck breast immediately, before the fat sets. How do you know whether to wait or not, and whether postponing is a clever trick or just proof of laziness? No need for an objective criterion. In the end you always know.

Cracking nuts or not

Alexander Grothendieck, who won the Fields Medal in 1966 (the equivalent of the Nobel Prize in mathematics) and who was an authentic genius recognized for his original intuition and copious discoveries, also uses this method. In mathematics there are no burned pans as such, but there are problems that catch, some of which stick for centuries and which whole generations scrub away at. Author of a monumental work, several thousand pages of which have yet to be explored, after having revolutionized algebraic geometry and opened the field to an army of researchers, Grothendieck turned his back forever on the mathematical community and went to live far away in a little village in the Ariège, devoting himself to meditation. His contribution to the problem of space, according to specialists, is as significant as that of Einstein. Both put space at the center of the history of the universe. I'm going to refer here not to the contents of his mathematical work—that would be beyond me—but to his method for resolving the most intractable difficulties. In addition to his mathematical work, Grothendieck left a substantial autobiography, still unpublished and available on the internet, entitled *Récoltes et semailles* (Reaping and Sowing). In it he describes the two main methods for addressing a problem.

Let us take, for example, the task of proving a theorem which remains hypothetical (which in some people's view is what mathematical work is all about). I can see two opposite ways of going about this. One is that of the hammer and the chisel, when the problem in question is seen as a big nut, hard and smooth, which you have to break in to to reach the nourishing flesh protected by the shell. The principle is simple: you place the cutting edge of the chisel against the shell and hit hard. If necessary you do the same in several different places until the shell breaks—and then you are happy. This approach is especially tempting when the surface of the shell has rough or knobbly places where one can get a grip. In certain cases it is obvious where these knobbly places are, in other cases we have to turn the nut every which way and inspect it carefully before finding a point of attack. The most difficult case is when the shell is perfectly and uniformly rounded and hard. However hard you hit it, the cutting edge of the chisel skids and scarcely scratches the surface and you end up exhausting yourself. Even so, muscle power and endurance will sometimes bring success.

This first method, as muscular as it is inelegant, is obviously not the one he prefers.

I could illustrate the second approach by keeping the image of the nut which has to be broken open. The first image that came to my mind just now is that of plunging the nut into an emollient liquid, perhaps simply water, and from time to time rubbing it so that the liquid works its way in and otherwise leaving time to do its job. The shell gets softer over weeks and months—when the time is ripe it is enough to give it a squeeze and the shell opens like a perfectly ripe avocado! Or again, you could leave the nut to ripen under the sun and the rain and even perhaps through the winter frosts. When the time is ripe a tender shoot coming from the flesh within will have broken through the shell, almost playfully— or to put it another way, the shell will have opened of its own accord to allow it through. The image that came to me a few weeks ago was quite different: the unknown thing that I had to know seemed to me like an expanse of land or dense rock, resisting penetration. You can hack away with picks or crowbars or even pneumatic drills: that's the first approach, the chisel one (with or without hammer). The other approach is that of the sea. The sea moves forward imperceptibly and silently, nothing seems to break, nothing moves, the water is so far away one can scarcely hear it . . . however, in the end it surrounds the recalcitrant material, and little by little it becomes a peninsula, then an island, then an islet, which ends up submerged, as if it was finally dissolved in the ocean, which stretches out as far as one can see . . . That's the "sea" approach, of submerging, absorbing, dissolving—the approach in which, if one is not very careful, nothing ever seems to happen: at each moment, each thing is so obvious and above all so natural that often one would scarcely bother to write it down, for fear of appearing to be inventing it, instead of tapping away with your chisel like everyone else . . .

This text is rather long, but the network of images that it proposes is so coherent, it deserves to be left intact. Two approaches, then: the first that of the hammer and chisel; the second that of the sea. The first goes straight at the difficulty and hits it, trying to break it come what may; the second, patient, elegant, widens our vision and allows time for the difficulty to resolve itself naturally and easily. It is not the difficulty that has changed nature, but the manner of approaching it that has solved it without effort. The full-frontal method of impatient people can work, but it remains essentially inelegant, which is enough to condemn it definitively in the eyes of a mathematician who is as much an aesthete as an intuitive.

Galloping past the obstacle

Resolving a difficulty is also an artistic problem; for instance, the musician faced with a score. When you perform a work you have no choice, you must play all the notes as written and follow the route you've been given. What do you do when you get stuck? Discussing editions of the pianist Alfred Cortot's work, Hélène Grimaud decries the suggestion to practice difficult sections of a piece—such as problematic thirds, fourths, or arpeggios—out of context and independently of the whole. She writes:

> For me this method is the perfect way of creating a problem where none existed and of inventing difficulties before they arise. When there is a real technical difficulty it is precisely the musical context that helps you overcome it, the context from which the Cortot editions would like to separate it. Rather like a horse that insists on jumping only the most difficult obstacle in a course, without the momentum derived from the beginning of the race and without being lured on by the remainder of his run...

After Grothendieck's sea image, we have Grimaud's image of the galloping horse. In each case the idea is not to focus directly on the difficulty, not to insist on resolving it in isolation, but to fit it into a bigger picture and put it into its place, so that it disappears as you go by, without stopping to look at it directly. Not to give it more importance than is necessary, not to accord it significance in the race. Above all not to insist. The pianist Glenn Gould had a comparable technique, which involved putting the radio and television on at full blast before he attempted a very difficult piece, so that he couldn't hear himself play. The block would immediately disappear; perhaps the mind, too busy with the background noise and incapable of thinking of the difficulty that usually blocked it, could no longer be frightened by it. The din thus liberated twofold, first by distracting the mind from its task and then by making any possible error completely undetectable.

Working with trepidation but without fear

The tightrope walker, Philippe Petit, describes his technique for overcoming a block: "If day by day, little by little, a stunt starts to pose problems for me, to the point where I can't use it, I have to think of an alternative movement to replace it in my show. Otherwise I might find myself having a panic attack." So there is no pressure, it's not a case of double or quits, the tightrope walker knows how to land on his feet; he has a backup solution. But that doesn't mean that he admits defeat. He continues to attempt the stunt "each time with more trepidation and stealth. I want the feat to stay and to feel I've conquered it." If the stunt continues to pose problems, he "flee[s] the field. But without the slightest fear." A strange situation, since he recognizes both "more trepidation" but "not the slightest fear."

Trepidation at the thought of messing up the stunt in training has in fact nothing to do with the fear of messing it up on the day of the show. You might even say paradoxically that this trepidation prevents fear, since thinking about the stunt completely fills his mind. Rather than of trepidation, which seems to be synonymous with fear, we should talk of extreme attention. In the end, the word "attention" implies both trepidation— just as when you shout "Watch out!"—and the opposite of fear, since rather than paralyzing us, well-focussed attention allows us to eliminate the danger and find a solution.

Keeping busy to avoid fear

"I am never afraid on the rope," says Philippe Petit, "I'm too busy." Action saves you from fear; there are so many things to do on the rope that there's no time for it. The problem comes before that. Imagination and passivity increase the sense of danger. When you have all the time in the world you always think about the worst. Philippe Petit's method consists of managing every detail of his performance in person: the preparation and transportation of the material, the installation of the cable and the choice of place; everything is organized like a heist. Usually he's doing something illegal, but rather than being an additional difficulty that is an essential part of the success of the "job." Concern about being arrested, found out, or recognized before he can launch himself on his rope enables him to not be afraid and to not think for one moment about what he is going to do. Illegality is not a detail. It allows him to not think about the actual crossing. Philippe Petit doesn't expressly say this. But that's probably also why he's so fond of these problems. While you're busy solving a problem you don't think about the drop. You solve each problem in turn, you give in to necessity. Giving in: what could be easier?

Every problem brings its own solution

When you've got a problem, don't think about solutions but think about the problem itself, love it as if it were a person, let it speak for itself. The solution will come once you have agreed to settle into it, and given up any idea of leaving it, rather than if you turn your back on it, hell-bent on getting away. Moreover, there is true joy to be found in the problem. Nothing is more exciting than a problem to be solved. It's a chance to exercise your imagination, your intelligence, your intuition. A problem is a hand reaching out toward you and every problem always brings its own solution, if you look at it the right way. Solutions spring up easily of their own accord. If several solutions present themselves, choose the simplest one. If they are all equally simple, go for the most elegant one. Elegance, explains Philippe Petit, is doing as little as possible. Imagine there's a ladder you need to take up three stories on the outside of a building. To take the ladder up you've got a rope. Though the usual way would be to tie lots of knots to make the ladder safe, Philippe Petit demonstrates on a model how he did it without tying a single knot. All he had to do was to slip a loop of the rope between the top bars of the ladder and then thread the ends of the rope through this loop. By this means the ladder is both held up by the rope and stabilized by its own weight when it's pulled up. Petit uses the ladder's shape to solve the particular problem it presents. He doesn't go against this shape, he uses it as it is. An obstacle is always a leverage point, that's the secret. As far as the weight of the ladder is concerned, there too he uses it to stabilize the object like the bob on the end of a plumb line, or like the weight hanging at the end of a pendulum. Each time, the tightrope walker uses the problem itself as the solution. And when he is walking on a rope with the help of a pole weighing up to 55 pounds, it's by using this weight, which would be a handicap for a beginner, as a means of anchoring himself on the rope, to sink into the rope and ground himself in it to keep a better balance. And sometimes an unforeseen difficulty presents an unforeseeable solution. When he was looking for the best place to pull off his stunt at the very top of the Twin Towers, Philippe Petit hurt his foot quite badly. He was forced to use crutches, and he returned to the entrance to the building cursing his handicap, convinced that it would make him much more likely to be recognized and to be hindered in his reconnaissance. But the opposite happened. The security guards, seeing him physically challenged, opened the doors, took care of him, and gave him much easier access. The difficulty had involuntarily become an unintended stratagem. Philippe Petit, though a master of disguise, hadn't thought of it himself, but given the chance he seized it.

Trusting the first time

Preparation is often confused with practicing. Excessive practice can also make you stale. By removing every risk, you still run the risk of reducing your desire and wearing out your concentration. You need to trust in the first time. Hélène Grimaud says: "I have never liked having a run-through of a work before an opening concert. Why would you have your first kiss in substandard conditions? A bad hall, bad acoustics, and average piano? The first time I refused a run-through of this kind, everyone told me it was suicide. I stuck to my guns, but each time I was amazed at the general hostility I incurred." Until the day when Martha Argerich, one of the greatest pianists in the world, said to her, "This idea of running through a work in advance is really ridiculous. It is the first time you play something that you really need to match what you've imagined during the many hours of work, preparation, and practice." Alain comes close to this idea when he says that you have to succeed at the first shot. The attention is a weapon that you mustn't use until you need it. Hélène Grimaud goes further: "The first time is often magical: nothing has happened to diminish the utopian idea that you had of the work. Your playing is bathed in an ephemeral and resplendent grace. The second time, you have to get back up there, and start again, this time with a full awareness of everything that can go wrong."

Finding the right gesture

Insisting, whether with the body or in thought, is always counterproductive. The more you force, the more you fail. Worse still: you might hurt yourself. Yannick Noah recognizes of course that "interiorizing a technique cannot be done without effort, but you must choose the most intelligent method and reject the less attractive aspects of the work." Mechanical repetition of a gesture does not really enable you to master it. You are bound to wear yourself out, but you may start to doubt yourself too.

> By repeating the gesture over and over the pupil ends up by reaching a decent success rate under ordinary conditions, but nothing proves that he will be able to maintain that under extreme conditions. It's better to take the time to intellectualize the gesture, to understand it and to imprint it once and for all on one's subconscious: it's explained to you, you test it, it's explained to you again if necessary, you test it again, and if you are certain that you've understood it that's enough—there's no point going on and on! Next!

Once you've understood, there's no point in insisting. It's like tuning a guitar. Once you've found the right pitch for a string you must stop looking. You would only detune it again by persisting. This brings us back to the question of the 10,000 hours. A purely quantitative approach to training, even if it includes the idea of "mindful practice," based on a conscious effort toward a precise goal, doesn't work. Noah says that it's enough for a "knot" to form in a player's head, and no one to come to his aid, for him to leave his body and just go through the motions of training. "Then he could spend five hours a day on court without getting any benefit from it. He will lose and then say 'I don't understand, I'm trying really hard, I trained really hard but I had an off day.'"

To undo this kind of knot, first of all you have to relax. Not insist. Not pull on the knot. Take up a comfortable position and start by breathing properly. Relaxation doesn't come directly; if someone tells you to relax you are going to tense up, and this takes us back to the law of the inversion of misdirected effort. Once again, you reach the goal indirectly by concentrating your attention on your breathing. If you breathe well, slowly and deeply, you cannot fail to relax. It happens all by itself.

Then, to make the right gesture, you have to begin by understanding it, imagining it, visualizing it. In *Chariots of Fire*, the trainer, Sam Mussabini, explains to the sprinter Harold Abrahams that he is confusing speed and haste: "Don't over stride!" It's enough, the trainer explains to him, to do two extra steps over a hundred meters, therefore smaller steps, in order to win. What you're after is spring, naturalness, and relaxation, rather than the effort of a huge leap. It's first and foremost a mental task, calling for imagination. "Visualization," Noah explains, "opens up as many perspectives as in-depth work, and is just as effective as hours of mechanical training." You can work at your technique without getting out of bed: you start by visualizing a wonderful place. Using the rhythm of your breath, you take possession of your body. You dissect the movement or the activity that you want to master. Then you visualize yourself executing the perfect gesture. This gesture imprints itself on the brain and can be modified at will.

> The aim of visualization is simple: to enter into the gesture. I have a very precise memory of Sampras at the French Open at the time of his marathon-like matches in 1996. He was so relaxed that gradually he just became *part of* the game. He served in this fantastically relaxed way, he was on top of every ball, he *was* the serve, he *was* the shot. He *was* tennis. And it was extraordinary to watch, because it's so rare that someone can relax their body to that extent. But as it happens, it was a matter of survival, because he was reaching the limit of his physical capacity. It seemed to me he was showing us tennis which only he could visualize.

Visualization is based on the association of the imagination with the body. If you imagine well, you act well. And mastery of a gesture will come not from physical repetition but rather from switching back and forth between imagination and action. "Once the gesture is accomplished, there's no point in repeating it 50,000 times. It's there. You've got it. It won't fly away. Even in an extreme situation." Maybe that's the most surprising part: a gesture learned in this way is so deeply known that it will always be available, even under stress. The advantages of this method are countless: you can carry on working even when you are injured. And you are free to imagine all kinds of situations. You are literally ready for anything. The same method can be found in the *Hagakure*, the manual of samurai ethics, which recommends imagining every combat situation, so as to be ready when the moment comes. Musicians draw on it too. Hélène Grimaud reports that at one point in her life her work took place less on the instrument than in her head. "I worked by thinking, by associating images, by mental projections and visions of architecture, and of colors. I steeped myself in them." Visualization, then, is not necessarily immediately followed by action. You can set it to one side, or let it seep into you. Noah recommends that when you are training and finding it difficult to be in the moment, you should above all not insist. "Sometimes a walk in the forest when you're relaxed and concentrating on the goal is much more useful than three hours of drills."

Taking a walk with Rousseau

Taking a walk is an art that consists of allowing walking to take over from thought and allowing your mind to wander. A true walk should have no goal other than itself. That way it will be much healthier. Rousseau tells us how his purest and most lasting moments of pleasure came to him while he was walking, strolling aimlessly, or lying in a boat, looking at the sky. This solitary meditation is based on an act of renunciation that, because it is sincere, turns out to be happy and fruitful. Reverie, meditation, walking, though it may not look like it, are never a waste of time. Ideas do not come because we pursue them, but because we are open to them. Once the mind is purified of its concerns, its tensions, clarity comes naturally.

The art of resting

Finally, the most important condition, the essential precondition of attention, is rest. André Breton tells us that before taking a nap, "Saint-Pol-Roux used to hang a sign on the door of his country house saying 'POET AT WORK.'" The surrealists relied on sleep and dreams to find inspiration, breaking the straitjacket of the day's binary logic. Recent scientific research confirms that sleeping allows the brain to work, or rather to infuse, absorbing both abstract information and new physical movements; sporting or artistic gestures, piano, tennis, or learning a language. Night not only brings counsel, it also opens new doors.

But to reap the benefits of sleep you must be able to sink into it. In a chapter devoted to insomnia, Alain defines the position of rest as "that in which there is no further to fall. The remedy is first to allow gravity to act, so that it has nothing left to act on. Become liquid." What wakes you up is the feeling of falling.

You must therefore find a position in which no part of your body can sink any lower. Otherwise the least movement becomes a warning and wakes us.

To become liquid is also to give up shaping any thoughts. Remember the sea, which teaches us that forms are not real, and which resists all our ideas. Knowing how to sleep means first of all sending our thoughts to sleep and stopping them from taking shape. Attending to your breath is a good way of achieving this. If necessary, the imagination comes to your aid. In particular, the imaginary world of water. Gaston Bachelard, author of the wonderful *L'Eau et les rêves* (Water and Dreams), lived in Place Maubert on the Boulevard Saint-Germain, which was a particularly noisy street. He tells us that one night, when he couldn't sleep because of the constant noise of traffic, he began to imagine that the noise of the cars was that of waves. Cradled by this friendly sound, he dropped off happily, and was able to slip effortlessly into a deep slumber.

10

The Power of Dreams

It's pointless to act against your will,
that is to say, against your dreams
GASTON BACHELARD

For many years, Alain Passard roasted meat. People came from all over the world to taste the meat dishes in his three-Michelin-star restaurant, L'Arpège, a stone's throw from the Rodin Museum and the gilded dome of the Invalides. He understood meat better than anyone, particularly how to cook it. He had learned the "art of fire" from his grandmother, an exceptional cook, who showed him how to always keep one eye on the flame and to listen carefully. "I can still hear her oven whistling when the fat began to sizzle at the bottom of the dish." To understand the song of fire you have to have perfect pitch. Cooking is a timeless art, with its own secrets. For example: "The burned surface is a whole art in itself. Cooking on a wood fire is a kind of cooking where the fire leaves a far more powerful imprint: you can taste the flame in it. A browned surface comes from a damper cooking, and that's different." It's like listening to a ceramicist or an alchemist talking. In his *La Psychanalyse du feu* (The Psychoanalysis of Fire), Gaston Bachelard has a similar recollection:

> Filling her cheeks and puffing into the steel tube, my grandmother would bring the smoldering flames back to life. Everything was cooked together: potatoes for the pigs, then better-quality potatoes for the family. A fresh egg would be cooked for me in the ashes. There was no timer for the cooking: the egg was cooked when a drop of water, often spit, evaporated on the shell. I was very surprised when I read recently that Denis Papin used to watch his pot using my grandmother's method.

Whether you're a physicist or a cook, the lesson of fire is always the same: you must give it your full attention. And such close attention will be generously rewarded. "If I was behaving myself," Bachelard goes on,

> they'd get out the waffle iron. Its grid pressed down on the blazing brushwood, as red as a gladioli head. And in a moment the waffle was in my apron, hotter to the fingers than to the lips. Then, indeed, I was eating fire, I was eating its golden flames, its smell, and even its crackling, as I crunched the burning waffle between my teeth. And in this way fire proves its humanity every time, providing the pleasure of a

kind of luxury, like a dessert. It doesn't just cook, it crusts, it gilds the cake. It gives form and substance to the festivities of men. As far back as you care to go, gastronomy wins over nutrition and it was in pleasure and not in pain that man discovered his spirit. Man is a creation of desire, not a creation of need.

Alain Passard could certainly sign up to this idea, since he is only able to work in a state of pleasure; ever since he was fourteen years old he has experienced cooking as a dream. But there was a certain point when meat lost all meaning and interest for him, and even began to disgust him. Was it those pictures of mad cows filling our screens? Or because of his relationship with the dead animal? Or because of blood? He'd had enough. The man who lived only for carving, larding, boning, browning, flambéing, cooking salt-crusted beef ribs, shoulders of lamb, and duck breasts, could no longer bear to look at or touch, let alone smell, animal flesh. He had lost all pleasure in it. His desire was thwarted. His joy had gone. His dream had become a nightmare. What happened to the flame? Alain Passard loved cooking so much, but he'd made up his mind: he had to give the whole thing up, right now. It was 1998. Farewell calves, cows, pigs. And above all, farewell L'Arpège.

A year later, Alain Passard returned. He had decided to change career. He had been a roaster of meat. Now he was a painter: "Look! Let's make a family, we'll take one color as the starting point. I like orange shades, and I'm going to have fun.

Watch, I'll make a bouquet—bam! Like a painter. Here's a little touch of green. Let's set that off with a leek. Look: here's my dish." A painter who makes bouquets—so a sort of florist. We can see this in his *Tarte aux pommes bouquet des roses* (Rose bouquet apple tart), a creation he is very proud of, and which demands a goldsmith's skill to roll the thin ribbons of apple into flowers: "Cooking is like the jeweler's craft... What counts is the hand, the gesture. It's important to have that sense of precision and exactness. In cooking, you have to know how to delicately hone your senses, as if you were a great parfumier." Creating correspondences, giving a color a taste, being at once a parfumier, a painter, a florist, a jeweler, a couturier, a sculptor, and a musician. Anything but a roaster of meat. Because, Alain Passard's big idea, his saving "eureka," which, though born of solitude and painful retreat, enabled him to come back firing on all cylinders, was to ditch the meat and keep the fire. From now on, the vegetable would be king. That's all he would cook. After all, one can cook a salt-crusted beetroot, celery can be smoked, onions flambéed, carrots grilled. Like a vegetarian Prometheus, he decided to steal fire from meat and apply it to vegetables. A mad and heretical idea for a three-star chef, almost an insult to French gastronomy, but that's what he decided. The meat nightmare was over; enthusiasm and the will to create were back. He was back, as he puts it, with a new touch, a new look, new flavors, new scents, different cooking sounds. And he had recovered his sense of pleasure. Anxiety over blood yielded to vegetable dreams. Vegetables mean earth, slow growth, the rhythm of the seasons, deep roots and the promise of fruit. Everything Bachelard calls "relaxing dreams." Dreams that speak to the ears of people worn out by city life, dreams made to be shared: "I grow my vegetables," Passard explains, "so I can tell a story, from plant to plate." Because in the heat of action he has become a gardener. Not just any gardener. There too reverie transforms *métier* into art. "It's the same mind-set as a winemaker's. When I talk about a beetroot or a carrot with the lads in the garden, we talk about them as we would about Chardonnay or Sauvignon. The idea is to make a vintage of vegetables and above all to make gardening the profession of the future." This is both a lovely dream and a dream of loveliness, in which the particularity of the soil and the wisdom of the seasons are more important than hydroponics and strawberries in January. In Alain Passard's world, you may hear such phrases as "the tomato harvest is a rendezvous," and at once it is clear that this means a rendezvous between lovers. It means the soil is a real thing and a vegetable is a real person.

Alain Passard's eyes are shining again, just like his grandmother's in front of the fire. He has rediscovered his taste for cooking, thanks to vegetables, and above all, which is the point I was coming to, thanks to the dreams that vegetables make possible. "Take away dreams," Bachelard writes in *La Terre ou les rêveries de la volonté* (Earth and Reveries of Will), "and you will weigh down the worker. Neglect the dreamlike power of work and you'll destroy the worker. Each kind of work has its own dream world, each substance worked upon brings with it its particular reveries. The dreamlike aspect of work is a necessary condition for the mental health of the worker." For work to be happy, it must be sustained by a dream. But be careful. Not a dream in opposition to reality, not a compensating dream of the Freudian kind, or a dream of greatness as with ambitious people, but an elementary reverie engraved on the material and in the gestures it makes possible, a reverie that plays with the powers of fire and the secrets of the earth. Every sincere worker is first and foremost a dreamer, and that is what makes his or her work easy, each of his or her efforts successful. When the imagination works in harmony with the hand, the whole being vibrates with the joy of making. Whether for a metallurgist or a cook, the fire gives light to their labors. The earth, meanwhile, bears both the dreams that issue from the will and those that come from relaxation. And nature is a generous goddess, working for you: "Harmonies," says Alain Passard, "create themselves. I don't have to say to myself: is that going to go with that? No. It's fine. Because it's produce that ripens together. The finest cookbook was written by nature. You just have to observe the calendar that nature has defined." If you follow the rhythms of nature you will rediscover the true sense of the word "work," as adventure, journey, conquest, but also as rest, since winemakers and gardeners know that trusting nature means letting her work and knowing when to let her rest.

"A farmer's muscular effort pulls up the weeds, but only sun and water can make wheat grow." The ultimate dream for Alain

Passard is for himself to be like the sun and water, to walk as lightly as possible upon the earth and to forget skill and return to what is natural.

This balance between the dreams of the will and those of rest is the true treasure that is hidden in the earth. Alain Passard admits this: "I have never felt so well as since I've had my gardens." Cultivating one's garden, the philosopher's advice and the alchemist's dream, allows you to see a beetroot as a precious stone and a potato as a golden nugget. Although I hated vegetables as a child and thought of them as a medical imposition, an unavoidable dietary inconvenience, the collateral damage of meat eating, I have to recognize that thanks to Alain Passard, I have experienced a revolution in taste, and that hearing him speak about vegetables has led me to think of them differently, as marvelous gifts rather than the recommendations of some dietician. What is more, you need only see him waiting every morning with his colleagues for the delivery of fruit and vegetables from his gardens: Passard respects the seasons, there will be no tomatoes after October 15, and yet every day is a feast day...

There are dreams inspired by fire and by earth, and there are also those inspired by water. For as far back as he could remember, Jacques Mayol always dreamed of the sea.

I often went diving with my brother Pierre. We had fun pretending to be pearl fishers and we dreamed of the extraordinary dives that we'd do one day in Tahiti and all kinds of other places around the world, as soon as we were old enough. We stayed in the water from dawn till dusk, discovering day after day the beauties of the deep, fish of every color and magnificent shells.

It was his mother who taught him to be at ease in water, introducing him to holding his breath at a very early age: "When she gently put my head under the water in our family bathtub, she was trying to teach me that the first thing you have to do to familiarize yourself with the world of the sea is to hold your breath."

Today his mother would be proud of him, and perhaps a little anxious as well. He's already fifty meters down, the depth at which the Boyle-Mariotte law, well known to deep sea divers, predicts the crushing of the lungs of the freediver who is not breathing air from bottles. This doesn't bother Mayol. He has already known for twenty years what is awaiting him: "It's a wonderful feeling at sixty meters, when you feel two huge hands squeezing you but without hurting, gently, making your blood flow to the lungs so that you can go even deeper. You mustn't be afraid of letting yourself go. And then you feel as though you are an integral part of the universe." These interthoracic spasms, followed by an extraordinary feeling of well-being, are called "blood shift" or "peripheral vasoconstriction," as mentioned in chapter 6. It's a rush of blood enriched with red corpuscles from the peripheral regions of the body to the noble organs, situated in the interthoracic cavity, and up to the brain. "On the one hand, this rush creates a sort of cushion that can resist the effects of pressure. On the other hand, it sets up a supply of fresh red corpuscles to those elements of the organism that most need it at that moment. This has been observed particularly in the case of whales, when they dive very deep." This blood shift, described by doctors as a physiological phenomenon, is for Jacques Mayol a much more dreamlike and personal experience. He literally puts his life in the hands of the sea. At the age of seventeen, Jacques signed up for the air force, dreaming of being a student pilot in a flight school in the United States. He ended up in Agadir, as a translator/flight controller in a control tower. It doesn't matter, because today he is flying in water, like an astronaut, but going down. He doesn't care about the sound barrier, because on November 23, 1976, just off the Isle of Elba, he broke the hundred-meter barrier. He remembers it as if it were yesterday: "I had a moment of delirious joy, a little like what Neil Armstrong must have felt when he set foot on the moon. A sort of nirvana, one hundred meters down." That was seven years ago. He was forty-nine years old. Now he is eighty meters down. In almost total darkness, broken only by the light beam from the diving weight. He thinks of Clown, the dolphin friend who has trained him so well. Even today he would have preferred a dolphin to lead him to the bottom, rather than a weight. He decides to remove his nose clip. The seawater immediately fills his nasal cavities. "More than ever before, I had, at that moment, the feeling of being transformed into a marine animal. I felt a vague drunkenness, as if unknown faculties were awaking deep within me." He broke the hundred-meter barrier without noticing. The rest happened as in a dream, as his attitude reveals: "Exactly eighty-four seconds after the beginning of my dive, the heavy weight hit the depth indicator with a boom." Dazzled by the lights, Jacques cannot make out the faces of Guglielmi and Araldi (his safety divers). He is extraordinarily calm. Noticing that one of the two metal buckles linking the resurfacing float to its gas bottle is slightly caught, he takes the time to free it. Then he takes hold of one of the little alcohol bottles on which the depth of 105 meters is written. He slips it under the top of his diving suit. His gestures are slow and completely relaxed. Then he gives a twist to the tap on the gas bottle and the float gently swells up with a hiss. A few more seconds to have a look around and he is on his way up, slowly at first, then faster.

At fifty meters, Jacques feels so good that he decides to let go of the grip of his resurfacing float and continues his upward journey by hand, completely relaxed, pulling himself up the cable with his arms. From time to time he looks upward, to where the light is getting stronger and more welcoming. His movements are open and synchronized. At thirty-five meters he stops for a moment, just to shake the hand of one of his divers, Guiseppe Alessi...

Another handshake at fifteen meters with another diver, and

another stop of a few seconds one meter below the surface to take out the little alcohol bottle that is his proof. Three minutes and fifteen seconds after entering the water, he breaks the surface and then almost immediately dives down to twenty meters again, to shake the hand of Guglielmi and Araldi, who at that depth have begun their long periods of decompression. Then he comes back on board and in a completely natural way, helps the sailors to haul in the cable with the 110-pound weight on the end. His face shows not the least sign of tiredness.

The most striking detail of this record dive is less the exploit itself than the facility with which Mayol accomplished it, as if he had all the time in the world, no hurry to get back to the surface, wanting only to extend his immersion as long as possible and to get back into the water as quickly as he could. That is less the ease of an athlete than the natural state of a dreamer. Mayol was in his element under the water. In *Water and Dreams*, Bachelard, who also associated water with love, gave a precise analysis of the world of aquatic dreams. What water promises is that life can float like a dream. If one compares the imaginary world of Jacques Mayol to that of his rivals, Robert Croft and Enzo Maiorca, radical differences are apparent. The American, Robert Croft, a military instructor in the navy, whose job was to teach recruits to get out of a submarine in difficulty on the seabed, developed his ability to hold his breath within the framework of his duties. Training took place in a water tower above the ground, thirty-six meters high, in Groton, Connecticut, a long way from the sea. The Italian, Enzo Maiorca, on the other hand, had an approach both athletic and human, which seemed to be founded on self-knowledge and an understanding of his own limits. "When holding your breath," he said, "you end up by assuming your exact own size, making your suit fit perfectly. When he is below water, the freediver sees himself in the depths, where he can, if he wishes, make a true X-ray of his heart and soul." The Frenchman, Jacques Mayol, was apparently the only one to maintain a real elementary dream, less about staying human in a foreign milieu than about melting into it, and becoming a dolphin. In *Homo delphinus*, the masterpiece that he compiled over many years, he sums up the path that seemed to have become his destiny: "Research into the diving reflex in humans. I am deeply convinced that this reflex, which we have from our origins, and which it should therefore be possible to bring to the surface again, even partially, from our genetic memory, is in total harmony with nature and excludes any artificial procedure."

Where Robert Croft imagines trying to escape from a submarine with his lungs as full as possible, and thinks of breathing according to the model of a military resource; where Enzo Maiorca steels himself not to breathe, following the model of athletic exploits; Jacques Mayol looks for relaxation and what is natural, following the model of the dolphin. A dream of difficulty overcome as opposed to a dream of facility, a dream of survival or human performance as opposed to a dream of becoming an animal. Who is right? Who is wrong? That is not the question. You don't have to judge the value of an imaginary system by its measurable output, nor reduce a dream to the role of adjunct to the sporting performance; you just have to notice the degree to which elementary dreaming can make effort easy and above all give life as a whole the fluidity of a dream. Someone who imagines himself as a dolphin will be as happy as a fish or, rather, a whale, in water. "Man," Jacques Mayol wrote, "will never die as long as he is able to dream. And the dream of *Homo delphinus* will live for as long as man protects the sea."

For Mayol it was dolphins; for Hélène Grimaud it's wolves. Two years after her serious moment of melancholy at the Festival de La Roque-d'Anthéron, the culmination of a depressive period in which she lost all pleasure in life and in playing, she had an unlikely and extraordinary encounter with a Canadian female wolf called Alawa. When she touched her,

> I felt this sudden spark, a discharge through my whole body, a single touch but which spread through my whole arm and chest and filled me with a kind of softness. Just softness? Yes, coming from her imperious way of being, and drawing out a mysterious song from me, the call of an unknown, primordial power. She had this strange fur, with very long hair, and intense yellow eyes, and in her company I felt happy, whole, absurdly young and strong.

This was in 1991 in Tallahassee, Florida, and from that moment on, nothing would ever be the same. Grimaud developed a passion for wolves, deciding she must know everything about them and opening a refuge for them. Thanks to wolves, she reconnected with her own intuition, and rediscovered a form of immediacy that she had lost through plunging herself into endless analysis of musical pieces, instead of playing them. A few years later she became an icon, "the pianist who runs with wolves," but she didn't care: she knew they were far more than just an accessory to her success. She knew there was an instinctive bond between them. That is, until the day when she was invited to Boulder, Colorado, to make a film with some wolves she didn't know, and was badly bitten. She admits:

To be honest, I had to fundamentally rethink my relationship with the wolves. I reached the painful realization that what had been happening until Boulder, this perfect symbiosis, my own animal side in harmony with that of the wolves, was completely abnormal, in the sense of being outside all norms. My unconscious, that feeling of complete invincibility, and sometimes even of immortality, that was my very essence, had imprinted my gestures with a kind of assurance which in the animal world only the dominant beasts possess. But I wasn't a female wolf, I was just a woman, and the rest, everything else, was just a privilege. So would I be able to reestablish this lost *innocence*? I realized I was asking the question the wrong way. The big mistake was to believe, "if I love him, he loves me too." The episode at Boulder taught me a lesson that I've applied ever since when I enter the wolves' enclosure. I always keep in mind the wolf's own terms, its rhythm and vision, not mine...I have learned to be extremely vigilant, and to be intensely engaged, down to my last fiber, my last neuron, in the relationship at that precise instant, as though it could slip away from me at any moment. And what is true for wolves is true for music too.

The wolf, first experienced by Grimaud as a dream, became a reality. But by adjusting to this painful new reality and losing her innocence, she acquired a new sense of presence and intensity. The call of the wolf first brought her out of her sadness by offering a dream, and then its bite brought her out of the dream, to show her reality. Hélène Grimaud realized the full meaning of this particular lesson when she was able to apply it to music, which she had lost her taste for. That was in Como, after a long, slow walk.

I sat on the stool and placed my hands on the keyboard and then, at last, I was what I hadn't been for a long time. I was alone with the instrument without any pressure and with nothing more at stake than the joy of playing. For once I could be in contact with works without doing anything other than reinventing them. For myself alone. For my pleasure alone. To find momentum, life, and joy again. So I played. I played without aim, without sadness, without sorrow. All that had vanished. I played for hours and hours. And after all those hours I saw the light.

That was the end of the perpetual discrepancy between the soul and its envelope, the end of being out of kilter with the world, the end of rumination. The wolves gave her back the pleasure of playing for nothing. The pure pleasure of playing, without a goal, by obliging her to return to reality. A difficult lesson for an unrepentant dreamer, lost in her reading, her scores, and her conviction that she was a wolf. "Now it makes me smile because I'm in a different place. I'm in space. I occupy it. I inhabit the gaps between wolves, music, and writing. And that's where I am at my best." Slipping into the gap, passing in between, weaving one's way through, what better definition could there be of playing? Where there is play, life can start to circulate again. But Grimaud did not renounce her dreams; she simply learned from them to be intensely attentive in real life.

Even if Hélène Grimaud, as Deleuze might say, was caught in a "wolf-becoming" that saved her life by restoring to her the possibility of metamorphosis, she never actually believed she was a wolf. She recognizes the boundary separating her from the animal world, and doesn't take her dream for reality. Jacques Mayol, who went much further—perhaps a bit too far—in his "dolphin-becoming," knew, however, that he was at best only a human amphibian, and that a total return to a watery existence was not possible. Others have not had such luck, or such wisdom. In Werner Herzog's *Grizzly Man*, a documentary, we meet Timothy Treadwell, who dreamed of becoming a bear and went to spend all his summers among the grizzlies in a wild region of Alaska. He said that he was ready to die for them, and that's precisely what he ended up doing. Eaten by a bear that, to be fair, he did not know. The power of dreams is always ambivalent. The power that inspires can also destroy. We can be broken by the dream running through us. But what are we to make of Treadwell? He died for his dream but he lived it out before dying. For thirteen years. A considerable length of time. But if we look more closely, wasn't this Californian bodyboard fan *surfing* bears rather than being their brother? Wasn't he hooked on the risk as much as on the animals themselves? And by living on their territory in the belief that he was protecting them was he not, on the contrary, lacking in respect toward them? Didn't he realize there was a price to be paid for crossing a border that both men and bears had respected for 7,000 years?

When Philippe Petit was balancing on his rope more than 400 meters up between the Twin Towers, perched like a bird, he says that he had a strange encounter. With a bird, in fact. Not a very friendly encounter. Probably curious about this intrusion into its space, the bird made a sufficient impression on the tightrope walker to convince him to obey the orders of the New York police and return to the human world below. Philippe Petit does not confuse the tightrope walker's dream and the dream of being a bird. The bird-becoming that he experienced has nothing to do with an illusion of changing into an animal.

Philippe Petit is a perfect example of the balance between dream and reality that separates unconscious madness from a feat accomplished. His preparation is unbelievably demanding.

For example, he trains himself to "remain balanced on one foot until the pain is no longer bearable, and then prolong this suffering for another minute before changing feet." Why does he put up with the unbearable when nothing forces him to? The answer is in the question: because nothing and nobody forces him to. "I believe the whip is necessary only when it is held by the student, not the teacher," he says. And he goes on: "The glory of suffering does not interest me."

His suffering is part of the story of realizing his dream. He doesn't seek pain for its own sake, he's not a masochist, he takes it for what it is: a sign that the body has reached a limit. And if you want to push back a limit you need to know exactly where it lies. Yannick Noah: "Pain is the athlete's barometer. The athlete likes to recognize signs of progress." It is only in this way that pain can be delicious. It gives proof that you are literally exceeding yourself. This enlargement of our being is a joy. The aim here is to engrave equilibrium upon the body. Philippe Petit: "When the positioning of each foot has become quite natural, the legs will have gained their independence, and your step will have become noble and sure." The skin suffers, but understands why. Changing skin comes at a price. "But I promise that when your feet slide to rest on a cable bed, you will astonish yourself with a smile of deep weariness. Look: on your sole there is what my friend Fouad calls the Line of Laughter. It corresponds to the mark of the wire." The aim of all these efforts is to make effort disappear. Effort is useful, inevitable, necessary. But it must be directed, limited, considered, and expert. And aim toward its own disappearance. Effort is only a scaffold, a halfway house toward equilibrium and repose. In the end, the tightrope walk must be pure pleasure and facility. And to those who say that is impossible, Philippe Petit replies: "Limits exist only in the souls of those who do not dream."

What's more, if the tightrope walker starts to suffer, it's never because he is trying too hard. Even when the rope begins to shake and you "want to calm it down by using force, you have to move smoothly without going against the rhythm of the rope." Being attentive to the rhythm of the rope, so you can tune in to its music, lessens the sensation of pain. Not only does the dream give meaning to the effort, it also has analgesic powers. When you are following your dream you don't experience pain in the same way. Petit considers training less of a trial than a hunt, a conquest: "You must not fall. When you lose your balance, resist for a long time before turning yourself toward the earth. Then jump. You must not force yourself to stay steady. You must move forward. You must win. Conquer!" You don't fall, you jump. Similarly, when you're chasing your dream, there is no place for tiredness: "Before setting foot on the ground, you must have reached a limit, however minimal: you are staking your reputation as a tightrope walker in order to win and so you have to leave your rope on a high, rather than because you're tired." There is therefore pleasure in effort. Far from being a stage on the road to a final dream of facility, the effort itself becomes, if not easy, then at least enjoyable. Philippe Petit, like Montaigne, might say: "Someone who only takes pleasure in pleasure, who only wins when he is at the top, who only likes hunting at the moment of the kill, has no business in our school." Pleasure, far from being reduced to the final moment of the kill, is spread throughout the hunt and coincides with it. The pursuit of happiness is already happiness itself. A dream worthy of the name is accomplished as one dreams it. If Philippe Petit is capable of walking without shaking, not on a "beam so broad that we could stroll along it," nor on "a plank wider than necessary," but on a simple rope stretched between the tops of the towers of Notre-Dame, if he seems in this way to refute both Montaigne and Pascal, this is not as a result of some new kind of philosophical wisdom, which is stronger than the imagining of vertigo, but of an even stronger imagining and an even grander reverie. The tightrope walker's dream is more powerful, vaster, and more euphoric than vertigo. Philippe Petit never had to struggle in vain against the fear of falling. This fear simply doesn't exist for him and has neither the time nor the occasion to come into being. It's not reason but imagination that triumphs over imagination: the dream cancels out the nightmare, quite simply by taking its place.

Yannick Noah agrees: "I don't believe in effort for effort's sake, I believe in making dreams come true." You play better when you know why you're playing or who you are playing for, when your effort has meaning. "Already as a junior player, I had won the title of champion of France, easy peasy, for a good reason: in the stands there was a girl from the Languedoc with a sad look, I couldn't get her out of my head. That day I pulled out all the stops and played much better than usual." Knights could always count on courtly love to give them wings in battle. Noah, who is still the only Frenchman to have won a Grand Slam tournament, has only ever done it once. He knows he could have done better, but nobody at the time told him how to go about it. What was he missing? He ended up by understanding it for himself, and too late. When you reach the summit, the problem is to find a new dream. Something else to conquer. An adventure rather than one more title to your name. "If I'd had in my head the metaphor Dan Millman is so fond of, describing a career in terms of a difficult climb up a high mountain, if I'd had the idea of setting off with a map like gold miners, I would certainly have accomplished greater things." Yes, you read correctly. What he lacked was not training or talent, but a metaphor to rekindle his desire and justify his efforts. If someone had told him that winning the French Open was only a step up and not a summit, that there was still a hard climb awaiting him, his life would paradoxically have been easier. Yannick Noah was hungry for images. It was his imagination that needed nourishment, not his willpower. As a trainer he has grasped this necessity and tries to feed the minds of players with rich and inspiring images. It's less the dream of victory than the reveries and focused imagination that work miracles. Imagining yourself as a gold miner when you're playing tennis might seem a bit beside the point, and yet the gold miner is on a quest, he knows no discouragement, he is ready to dig as deep as he must to find the seam. Gold, as alchemists knew, is the fruit of effort. Gold,

Olympic or physical, is always a distant dream requiring an effort to go deep and extract from the earth. On the one hand, you have the mountain as dream of air and ascent; on the other hand, gold, a dream of earth and the depths. It is always beneficial, Bachelard says, to offer images to an impoverished heart. The imagination dominates the life of the emotions. What Yannick Noah has created in the French Davis Cup team is a real Copernican revolution linking happiness and performance. Contrary to a long and ongoing tradition that characterizes happiness as the outcome of performance, he has adopted the opposite approach, which consists of starting from happiness and well-being to facilitate the performance. Performance is no longer an aim, it is an indirect consequence of happiness. You reach your goal without aiming for it. The dream is no longer simply a horizon, it's a state that you look for in order to play "as in a dream."

Not everyone, you tell me, can be a champion tennis player, freediver, tightrope walker, or pianist. And that's where I wish to bring this book to its close, sitting comfortably in an armchair with Gaston Bachelard, the philosopher of reverie and happy imagination. For anyone, as he explains, can be a champion in their imagination. There is nothing stopping you. No competition, no adversaries, no obstacles.

In other words, you don't have to dive a hundred meters down to be happy, it's enough just to dive into the imaginary. Someone who imagines well will live well, and is better preparing themselves for an act of will. Careful, though—imagination is not a compensatory or escapist dream, it's an energizing reality. Images are true accelerators of the psyche; they set the mind on fire. When you live out images sincerely, you feel them, you experience them. And you can do that lying on your bed, on a walk, in a train, in a plane, wherever you like. Obviously if you want the imagination to prosper, it's best if you have nothing to do. This workout for the imagination, which consists of imagining an effort in a lyrical manner, allows you, says Bachelard with some humor, to "tone your whole being without risking the muscular betrayal that comes from the usual gymnastic exercises." Of course, imaginary effort is anything but muscular. You won't thoroughly energize your being by pushing yourself physically. Ordinary gymnastics remain superficial. An athlete will not attain peak condition just by training more but by finding inspiring images. Hélène Grimaud rediscovered the joy of music not by forcing herself to play the piano but via the route of the "animal dream." "You don't become a *weightless* soul from one day to the next," warns Bachelard. "Pleasure is effortless and easy, but you must learn to be happy." You know the road, though. It is neither steep nor difficult. There it is, out ahead of us, or rather inside us. You simply have to imagine it. Alain Passard saved his three stars and his life as a chef not by forcing himself to cook meat, but by taking a step back, giving up his activity, and refreshing his imaginary world through contact with the earth. We believe, like Bachelard, that "the lines of the imagination are the real life lines, those that are the hardest to break. Imagination and the Will are two aspects of the same deep-seated force. The man who can imagine can exercise the will."

I remember when I was a child dreaming about the Tour de France before I knew how to ride a bike. I had a bike with training wheels. I used to watch Bernard Hinault on television, pedaling away. And then I would imitate him outside our house. If I got the angle right, and looked only at my shadow, I couldn't see the training wheels. Soon, by dint of imagination, I found the courage to take them off. I fell off a few times to start with, but the pleasure was greater than the pain. I was no longer trembling with fear; I was beaming with joy. This was it! I could ride a bike! A moment before, I couldn't. The next moment I could. Because, in a certain way, I already knew how to; I had already done it in a dream. Far from taking me away from my goal, reverie allowed me to reach it. Eureka! Anybody submerged in the imagination experiences a surge called hope. Bachelard says:

> For a task that is fairly clear and of a certain duration, you should probably think before acting, but you must also dream a great deal before even beginning to think. In this way our most productive decisions are related to nocturnal dreams. At night, we return to the land of rest with confidence, and we act out our confidence in our sleep. If you sleep badly you cannot have self-confidence. We might think of sleep as an interruption of our consciousness, but in fact it

binds us to ourselves. A normal dream, a true dream, is thus often the prelude and not the sequel to our active life.

It's not just night but also dreaming that brings counsel. Good dreams lead to good decisions.

Now you know what you have to do.

In Conclusion

The horizon is not a point, it is a continent
PHILIPPE PETIT

I began this book in Paris, and I continued it in Draguignan, but I wrote most of it in Greece, on the islands of Naxos, Syros, and Tinos, and then in Athens. The ever-present sea, frequent visits to its depths, the gentle warm air cooled by the wind, lovers' walks in the hills, the hospitality of friends and strangers, the example of vines and fig trees, which, without needing watering, bear delicious fruit—all this within arm's reach enabled me, I must admit, to work more easily than in Paris. Facility also comes from circumstances. This book is not exactly what I dreamed I would write—it's less complete, less perfect—but it exists, and in writing it I have tried to apply all the precepts that it contains, including renouncing perfectionism. If something of the happiness that came from the writing of it has survived into the reading of it I will have achieved my goal without making too much of an effort or reflecting or even aiming at it. If, as you've read through it, you've gleaned some new images, new approaches, and new ideas, that's great. They are only suggestions. It's only an airport book. But is something you glance through, sitting comfortably in an armchair, less valuable than something that you strain to learn, nailed to a chair in a classroom? I hope I have convinced you of the contrary.

"One day," says Roustang,

> a man weighed down by concerns about himself, who had reached a point where he was disgusted with himself, came to see me to be set free. After a few minutes' conversation I told him to stand up and take a step. Given this order, which he neither discussed nor deferred, he acted without thinking. He was suddenly freed from the anxiety of looking at himself and knowing what he was doing. His tortured face relaxed and he felt huge relief. Having for several minutes enjoyed a tranquility he hadn't experienced for a long time, he judged that this change, which had taken place without a struggle, was not possible, that it was just too simple. As he was telling me how astonished he was, I shared with him my own astonishment. He didn't come back, and must have returned to his demons. I only hope that he didn't forget what occurred. Perhaps it's a vain hope. He had experienced

the abolition of the distance between intention and action,
but he couldn't bear it.

I remember, when I was starting out on my literary studies, that
I had a moment of discouragement. Several, in fact. Why waste
one's youth studying? Paul Nizan's famous phrase—"I've been
twenty. Let no one tell me it's the happiest time of one's life"—
sank its teeth into me in the gray light of Paris. As a boarder
at Louis le Grand lycée, I was drowning in books, Latin trans-
lations, and essays. Shut away in a dormitory room, with a surface area of precisely 5.8 square meters, bent fourteen hours a
day over a classroom table or a plank serving as a desk, I would
yearn for those hours spent running or biking along the beaches
of Hyères, swimming out to the buoy at 300 meters, playing
tennis, soccer, frisbee, taking wind-surfing lessons, going to the
karate club. I would dream of Albert Camus, goalkeeper, fling-
ing himself into the warm dust of a soccer pitch in Algiers before diving into the Mediterranean, and everywhere I would
meet the shadow of Sartre sitting in the Café de Flore, lost in a
fug of concepts and cigarettes, hesitating between Being and
Nothingness. The days of a happy, active body were over. Paris
was all intellect and cold abstraction. What a pity! I had no time
now for sport. And none yet for love. Nor for writing. One day,
perhaps. And that's when I found, slipped into my pigeonhole,
a pamphlet for a course in karate being held very close to the
lycée, on Rue Malebranche. Beneath a portrait of Master Funa-
koshi, the founder of karate, was a phrase by Alain that sounded

at once like a commentary, a self-evident fact, and a promise: "The key to action is getting down to it."

So, in conclusion, I propose the following as a first experience on the journey to facility: as soon as you finish reading these lines and have closed the book, get up and take a step. Without thinking. Without hesitating. Now.

Bibliography

Many of the texts used in writing this book have not been translated into English. However, this is a selection of things I read and watched that inspired and informed my writing, and which you can discover for yourself in English.

Further Reading

Alain
On Happiness, tr. Robert D. Cottrell and Jane E. Cottrell, Northwestern University Press (1973)

Gaston Bachelard
Air and Dreams: An Essay on the Imagination of Movement, tr. Edith R. Farrell and C. Frederick Farrell, Dallas Institute of Humanities and Culture (1988)

René Descartes
Discourse on Method and the Meditations, tr. F. E. Sutcliffe, Penguin (1968)

David Epstein
The Sports Gene: Talent, Practice and the Truth About Success, Yellow Jersey (2014)

Malcolm Gladwell
Outliers: The Story of Success, Penguin (2008)

Hélène Grimaud
Wild Harmonies: A Life of Music and Wolves, tr. Ellen Hinsey, Riverhead Books (2006)

Michel de Montaigne
The Complete Essays, tr. M. A. Screech, Penguin (1993)

Philippe Petit
On the High Wire, tr. Paul Auster, W&N (2019)
To Reach the Clouds, Pan Macmillan (2002)

Jean-Paul Sartre
Being and Nothingness: An Essay on Phenomenological Ontology, tr. Sarah Richmond, Routledge (2018)

Stendhal
Love, tr. Gilbert Sale and Suzanne Sale, Penguin (1975)

Simone Weil
The Need for Roots: Prelude to a Declaration of Duties Towards Mankind, tr. Arthur Wills, Routledge (2002)
Waiting for God, tr. Emma Craufurd, Harper Perennial (2009)

Further Watching

David Gelb, *Chef's Table: France*, Episode 1: "Alain Passard," Netflix (2016)

Werner Herzog, *Grizzly Man* (2005)

James Marsh, *Man on Wire* (2008)

Acknowledgments

to Elsa, for her trust and patience

to Honorine, for her wisdom and international flair

to Maïté, for her support and giving up her holidays

to Yann, for his close reading

to Helen, for her fine and subtle translation

to Patrick, for his careful rereading

to Louisa, Penny, and the whole Profile team for enabling this French raft to cross the Channel with relative ease

to Alexis, for having told me about François Roustang and Alexander Grothendieck

to Christophe, for having introduced me to *Le travail intellectuel* to André, for having introduced me to Deleuze while playing tennis

to Hubert, for having made me take Alain seriously while drinking at L'Écritoire

to Jean-Henri, for his unfailing affection

to Jean, for having spoken to me of his friendship with Bachelard and offered me his own

to Vanessa, for having got her bac without aiming for it

to Gilles and Françoise, for shared pleasure and retsina

to Miltos and Irini, for hospitality and the lunar eclipse

to Yorgos, for grapes, tomatoes, and figs from his garden on Naxos

to Michaelis, for grilled grouper in Syros

to Aris, for the conversation about wine on Tinos

to Alain Passard, for a happy Christmas at L'Arpège

to my parents, for their love

to my children, for their vitality

to Laura, for the look in her eyes and everything else